Springer Theses

Recognizing Outstanding Ph.D. Research

Aims and Scope

The series "Springer Theses" brings together a selection of the very best Ph.D. theses from around the world and across the physical sciences. Nominated and endorsed by two recognized specialists, each published volume has been selected for its scientific excellence and the high impact of its contents for the pertinent field of research. For greater accessibility to non-specialists, the published versions include an extended introduction, as well as a foreword by the student's supervisor explaining the special relevance of the work for the field. As a whole, the series will provide a valuable resource both for newcomers to the research fields described, and for other scientists seeking detailed background information on special questions. Finally, it provides an accredited documentation of the valuable contributions made by today's younger generation of scientists.

Theses are accepted into the series by invited nomination only and must fulfill all of the following criteria

- They must be written in good English.
- The topic should fall within the confines of Chemistry, Physics, Earth Sciences, Engineering and related interdisciplinary fields such as Materials, Nanoscience, Chemical Engineering, Complex Systems and Biophysics.
- The work reported in the thesis must represent a significant scientific advance.
- If the thesis includes previously published material, permission to reproduce this must be gained from the respective copyright holder.
- They must have been examined and passed during the 12 months prior to nomination.
- Each thesis should include a foreword by the supervisor outlining the significance of its content.
- The theses should have a clearly defined structure including an introduction accessible to scientists not expert in that particular field.

More information about this series at http://www.springer.com/series/8790

Mohamed Mahmood

Does Digital Transformation of Government Lead to Enhanced Citizens' Trust and Confidence in Government?

Doctoral Thesis accepted by
Brunel University London, London, UK

Springer

Author
Dr. Mohamed Mahmood
Brunel Business School
Brunel University London
Uxbridge, London, UK

Supervisor
Prof. Vishanth Weerakkody
Management Information Systems
and Governance, Faculty
of Management and Law
University of Bradford
Bradford, UK

ISSN 2190-5053 ISSN 2190-5061 (electronic)
Springer Theses
ISBN 978-3-030-01758-3 ISBN 978-3-030-01759-0 (eBook)
https://doi.org/10.1007/978-3-030-01759-0

Library of Congress Control Number: 2018957668

This Springer imprint is published by the registered company Springer Nature Switzerland AG
The registered company address is: Gewerbestrasse 11, 6330 Cham, Switzerland

Supervisor's Foreword

Citizen trust and confidence in government are declining. E-government has been proposed as a means of reversing this trend by enabling the true transformation of government and improved performance. However, despite extensive investments of time and resources, e-government initiatives have largely failed to fulfil expectations. In this work, Mohamed Mahmood develops a novel conceptual model that provides a reference for planning the true digital-enabled transformation of government. This conceptual model is validated based on a survey of citizens of the Kingdom of Bahrain, which is highly ranked among Gulf Cooperation Council (GCC) countries in terms of the use of information and communications technology (ICC).

An important contribution of this work is that it is the first to investigate the relationship between the transformation of government and citizen trust and confidence in government from the perspective of citizens. The failure of e-government initiatives may be attributable in part to a focus on technical aspects (e.g., digitization and web-enabling of processes) rather than the core functions of government, as well as a lack of agreement on a common set of factors contributing to the decline in citizen trust and confidence in government. Mahmood's study finds that e-government and technology are not sufficient for achieving the true transformation of government and, in turn, reversing the decline in citizen trust. Government transparency and accountability as well meeting citizens' expectations and demands are identified as additional important factors.

Moreover, the validation of the conceptual model in the Kingdom of Bahrain confirms that digital-enabled transformation of government initiatives are working well in this country. This success is attributable to the small size and relatively homogeneous demographic composition of Bahrain, the relative maturity of its digital government initiatives, and the complete commitment of the government to these initiatives.

By deviating from standard techno- or user-centric theories, Mahmood's novel conceptual model provides a fresh new approach to understanding how digital-enabled transformation of government can enhance citizen trust and confidence in government, improve the government-citizen relationship, and increase the adoption of digital government services.

Bradford, UK
May 2018

Prof. Vishanth Weerakkody
Associate Dean, Planning
and Resources, Interim

Abstract

Over the years, citizens' trust and confidence in their governments has continued to decline and digital government is expected to reverse this trend. An enormous amount of money has been spent, worldwide, on electronic government initiatives that are focused on improving performance, reducing costs and enhancing citizens' trust and confidence in their governments. Yet, of the many initiatives that have been implemented, very few have achieved the real transformation of government (i.e. fundamental changes to the way core functions of government are performed to achieve noticeable gains in performance and efficiency). As such, there is a need to understand how the transformation of government as a construct affects citizens' trust and confidence in government in the presence of factors such as government performance and citizen satisfaction. This research empirically investigates the influence of digital transformation of government on citizens' trust and confidence in the context of the Kingdom of Bahrain. Bahrain is a top ranking country in terms of use of ICT in the Gulf Cooperation Council (GCC) region.

A conceptual model was developed and validated using an online survey targeting randomly citizens of the Kingdom of Bahrain. Based on 313 responses, the findings of this research suggest that citizens' trust and confidence in their government is positively influenced by the transformation of government, mediated by government performance and citizens' satisfaction. The study found that e-government and technology are not enough for achieving a real transformation of government, and therefore, in tackling the decline in citizens' trust and confidence in government. Other factors were found to be important in this equation, including transparency and accountability of government functions and activities in meeting citizens' expectations. The research offers multiple policy implications and theoretical contributions, in addition to helping understand how digital transformation of government can enhance citizens' trust and confidence in government, improve government-to-citizen relationship, and increase the adoption of digital services offered by governments. From a policy perspective, this research offers a validated conceptual model that can be used as a frame of reference when planning ICT-enabled transformation projects in government. From a theoretical context, this study is the first to investigate the relationship between the transformation of government and citizens' trust and confidence in government.

Declaration

Some of the material contained herein has been presented in the following publications:

Journal Papers: Published, Under Review and Rejected with Recommendations

[J4] Mahmood, M., Weerakkody, V. and Chen, W. (2017) 'The Role of ICT in the Transformation of Government and Citizen Trust', *Journal of Public Administration Review.* (Under Review)

[J3] Mahmood, M., Weerakkody, V. and Chen, W. (2017) 'The role of ICT in Transformation of Government and its Influence on Citizens' Trust', *Management Information Systems Quarterly.* (Rejected)
Although the submitted manuscript to the MISQ was rejected, it went through a full review process that lasted around 3 months and involved 5 reviewers (Senior Editor, Associate Editor and Three Reviewers). The subject and the identified knowledge gap in the submitted manuscript were found to be interesting by the 5 reviewers. However, the paper was rejected with positive comments and the authors were advised by the editor to submit an enhanced version of the manuscript (taking into account the comments and proposed suggestions) to a public administration journal such as the Journal of Public Administration Research and Theory (JPART) and Public Administration Review (PAR); Hence J4.

[J2] Mahmood, M., Weerakkody, V. and Chen, W. (2016) 'The Influence of Transformed Government on Citizens' Trust', *Journal* of *Information Technology for Development.* (Awaiting final acceptance following the fifth review of the manuscript).

[J1] Mahmood, M. (2016) 'Enhancing Citizens' Trust and Confidence in Government through Digital Transformation', *International Journal of Electronic Government Research,* Volume 12(1), pp. 99–110.

Conference Papers: Accepted and Published

[C3] Mahmood, M., and Weerakkody, V. (2016) 'Factors Affecting Citizens' Trust and Confidence in Government and Its Relation with Transformation of Government', *Proceedings of the 22nd Americas Conference on Information Systems (AMCIS-16).*

[C2] Mahmood, M. (2015) 'Enhancing Citizens Trust and Confidence in Government through Digital Transformation', *pre-ICIS workshop on eGovernment, 2015 International Conference on Information Systems (ICIS 2015).*

[C1] Mahmood, M., and Weerakkody, V. (2014) 'Digital government diffusion in Bahrain—The role of trust and its influence on adoption', *Proceedings of the 11th European, Mediterranean & Middle Eastern Conference on Information Systems (EMCIS 2014).*

Ph.D. Symposium Papers: Accepted and Presented

[S3] Mahmood, M., Weerakkody, V. and Alaali, M. (2017) 'The Influence of Transformed Government on Citizens' Trust', *Ph.D. Symposium.* Bahrain (the 8th Doctoral Symposium 2017). (**Best Paper Award**)

[S2] Mahmood, M., Weerakkody, V. and Alaali, M. (2016) 'The role of Trust and Its Influence on E-Government Adoption', *Ph.D. Symposium.* Bahrain (the 7th Doctoral Symposium 2016).

[S1] Mahmood, M., Weerakkody, V. and Alaali, M. (2015) 'Citizens' Trust and Confidence in Government and Its Relation with Transformation of Government', *Ph.D. Symposium.* Bahrain (the 6th Doctoral Symposium 2015). (**Best Paper Award**)

Appreciation and Recognition

[1] Winner of the Best Paper Award at the 6th Doctoral Symposium 2015.
[2] Following presenting successfully the paper titled "Factors Affecting Citizens' Trust and Confidence in Government and Its Relation with Transformation of Government" at the 22nd Americas Conference on Information Systems (AMCIS-16), the Journal of Information Technology for Development invited the Authors of this paper to submit an extended version of the AMCIS-16 paper.
[3] Winner of Best Paper Award at the 8th Doctoral Symposium 2017.

Acknowledgements

Praise be to Allah, the Almighty, the Cherisher and Sustainer of the Universe, and peace and blessings be upon his Prophet Mohamed.

First and foremost, I would like to thank my Ph.D. supervisor, Prof. Vishanth Weerakkody, for his excellent supervision throughout my Ph.D. His guidance enabled me to unitize my abilities towards getting things done, despite it being hard for me to work on the delegated actions at certain times. Throughout my Ph.D., he was available for supervision even across countries, which made my Ph.D. smooth and enjoyable. His encouragement and inspirations kept me motivated through the difficult phases of my Ph.D. I hope to maintain this relationship with my supervisor to produce more competitive work in future.

Furthermore, I greatly appreciate Prof. Mansoor Alaali, my second supervisor. His continued feedback helped me a lot through the Ph.D. journey, despite his busy schedule as the President of the Ahlia University.

I owe special thanks to my mother for her continuous prayers and endless support. She always wanted to see the day I complete this journey successfully. Moreover, my greatest thanks to my sister and family members for their never failing support, which has been a great source of motivation in this journey. My special thanks to Ms. Esra for being with me all the way, without whom, I would not have completed this journey. I cannot find proper words to express my appreciation for Esra.

I extend my thanks to all of my friends for their continuous encouragement, support and prayers; special words of gratitude go to Dr. Khalid, Marwan, Ahmed Bukhowa, Hisham and Abdullatif for being with me through this entire process.

Lastly, I would like to thank my country, Kingdom of Bahrain, for being my pride throughout my Ph.D. journey.

Contents

Chapter 1
Introduction

1.1 Introduction

This chapter provides an overview of the research covering the rationale and motivations for conducting it, identifies the gap, research questions, aim and objectives as well as the reasons for selecting the Kingdom of Bahrain for conducting the empirical work for the research. This research contributes to the growing body of knowledge and offers a number of implications for policy makers and practitioners. A quantitative research methodology is employed for the research along with adopting an online survey that was distributed randomly to citizens living in Bahrain. Structural Equation Modeling (SEM) was chosen as a multivariate technique and Confirmatory Factor Analysis (CFA) and path analysis were performed on the empirical data that was collected.

This chapter is structured as follows. Sections 1.2 and 1.3 provide a background of the research and presents the research problem and gap. This is followed by the research aim and objectives in Sect. 1.4. In Sect. 1.5, the significance of the research is described. Then, in Sect. 1.6, the employed research methodology selected for this research is highlighted. The thesis structure is presented in Sect. 1.7 and finally, Sect. 1.8, summarizes the overall chapter.

1.2 Research Background

An enormous amount of money has been spent worldwide on electronic or digital government initiatives. For example, the cost of e-government as of 2014 in the United States was 36.65 billion dollars since 1992, in South Korea it was 1.6 billion dollars since 2003 and it was 0.18 billion dollars in Russia since 2002 (Mukhoryanova et al. 2016). When comparing these figures to the early 2000s, e-government spending in the UK for the year 2001 was US$520 million, while it

M. Mahmood, *Does Digital Transformation of Government Lead to Enhanced Citizens' Trust and Confidence in Government?*, Springer Theses,
https://doi.org/10.1007/978-3-030-01759-0_1

was US$189 million in India (Basu 2004). As per the digital governance project database released by the World Bank in January 2017, 1129 investment-lending projects were funded by the World Bank in 135 countries around the globe since 1995 with a total amount of US$292,677 million.

The main purpose behind this global spending was to improve performance of governments, save costs and improve citizens' trust in their governments through digital transformation. However, despite this tremendous spending on digital government initiatives, the literature shows that citizens' trust and confidence in government is still in decline and further e-participation in digital services is still considered as a main challenge as highlighted by the United Nations E-Government Survey Reports released in 2012, 2014 and 2016. This leads to the fact that e-government did not work as planned and meet expected outcomes (Bannister and Connolly 2011; Gunawong and Gao 2017; Kim et al. 2009; Miyata 2011; Morgeson et al. 2011; Rodríguez Bolívar et al. 2016; Weerakkody et al. 2009; Welch et al. 2005). The increasing number of failed projects further confirms that e-government has failed to influence public engagement and increase citizens' trust in their governments. For instance, in the UK the government wasted several billion pounds on projects that were cancelled or failed to achieve stated objectives. Examples include the C-Nomis project (The Economist, Feb 2008), the e-borders system (£224 million), BBC digital video archive system (£100 million), Ministry of Justice back-office project (£56 million), NHS's National programme for IT (£10 billon) (The Guardian, 19 August 2014), Universal Credit (£425 million) (NewStatesman, 14 April 2014) and Common Agricultural Policy Delivery Programme (£642 million since 2005) (House of Commons, Feb 2017).

As a consequence of these failing digitally influenced government projects—for which a lot of money have been spent, public trust and confidence in governments in most countries has continued to decline during the last decade (Bean 2015; Edwards 2015; Morgeson et al. 2011; Teo et al. 2008; World Employment and Social Outlook Trends 2015, 2016, 2017). Yet, there is also evidence to show that there are some countries in the world where people still continue to have trust and confidence in their government, for instance, countries in south Asia and Sub-Saharan Africa (World Employment and Social Outlook Trends 2015). The reasons for such levels of trust are not clearly outlined by the International Labour Organization (ILO) in its report; however, from the themes of the report and the flow of sections, they can be related to social unrest, social conditions, rising inequalities, employment dynamics, income inequality and economic growth (World Employment and Social Outlook Trends 2015). Despite such isolated instances of certain countries where citizens seem to have trust and confidence in their governments, there is a broad consensus among researchers about the growing trust deficit and decline in confidence of people in their governments in general (Bovens and Wille 2008; Job 2005; Nye 1997; Scharpf 1999), reasons for which seem to be unclear. Studies have shown that this decline in citizens' trust in their government has contributed to lack of citizens' engagement and use of e-government systems that have been implemented as part of the transformative agenda in many countries (Bannister and Connolly 2011; Morgeson et al. 2011;

Teo et al. 2008; Tolbert and Mossberger 2006; West 2004). Yet, few studies have investigated the factors that contribute to this decline in trust and the relationship between transformation of government and citizens' trust and confidence in government.

1.3 Research Problem and Gap

Although literature shows that, some work has been done to understand the decline in trust and confidence in their government; this work has largely focused on technical, service quality, usability and adoption aspects of ICT enabled transformation projects in government with limited impact on practice. For instance, e-government was viewed as a solution to improve performance, transform governments, reduce costs and reverse this decline (Morgeson et al. 2011; Teo et al. 2008; Tolbert and Mossberger 2006). Yet, as outlined earlier, heavy investments in e-government and associated digital transformation projects have failed to meet the expected results. According to the United National Surveys 2012, 2014 and 2016, the levels of citizens' participation and adoption of digital government services is considered as one of the main challenges around the globe. As outlined by the UN and other normative studies, of the many projects that have been implemented around the world, very few have achieved real transformation of government (i.e. fundamental changes to the way core functions of government are performed to achieve noticeable gains in performance and efficiency) (Bannister and Connolly 2011; Gunawong and Gao 2017; Kim et al. 2009; Miyata 2011; Morgeson et al. 2011; Omar et al. 2017; Rodríguez Bolívar et al. 2016; Weerakkody et al. 2009; Welch et al. 2005).

The decline in public trust in government as well as the failing e-government projects has attracted the attention of a number of researchers due to the important role it plays in understanding citizens' behaviours towards their governments. For instance, some literature has tended to investigate certain components of citizens' experiences in e-government in isolation, which does not take into account the inherent complexities as well as the possible influence of many potential relationships amongst the factors that contribute to citizens' experiences (Morgeson et al. 2011). Similarly, it is found in the literature that there is a lack of agreement on a common set of factors that contribute to the decline in trust and confidence of people in their governments (Bannister and Connolly 2011; West 2004). Some of the factors which have been identified in the literature that influence citizens' trust and confidence are: technology (Morgeson et al. 2011; Tolbert and Mossberger 2006), transparency (Bannister and Connolly 2011; Kim et al. 2009), accountability (Bannister and Connolly 2011; Kim et al. 2009), citizens' expectations (Morgeson and Petrescu 2011; Morgeson et al. 2011), government performance (Bouckaert et al. 2005; Morgeson et al. 2011; Van de Walle and Bouckaert 2003; Van de Walle et al. 2008), citizens' satisfaction (Bouckaert et al. 2005; Morgeson et al. 2011; Teo et al. 2008; Van de Walle and Bouckaert 2003; Van de Walle et al. 2008) and transformation of government (Bannister and Connolly 2011; Waller and Weerakkody 2016; Zwahr et al. 2005). Noticeably, many of the identified factors in the literature are discussed in conjunction with transformation of government (Al-Shboul et al. 2014; Mahmood 2016; Siddique 2016). Yet, several studies have confirmed that there is a need to examine new determinants of government performance and citizen satisfaction, which have not been considered in the literature yet—for instance determinants of e-participation and satisfaction of citizens' in e-participation (Alharbi et al. 2016; Morgeson 2013; Reddick and Anthopoulos 2014). This argument could be extended to government transformation as a determinant of government performance and citizen satisfaction.

The term "transformation of government" is a complex one and it is hard to find a common definition for it in the literature. Accordingly, it should be dealt with carefully in any research. The literature shows that transformation of government has the potential to reverse the decline in citizens' trust and confidence in government (Bannister and Connolly 2011; Waller and Weerakkody 2016; Zwahr et al. 2005). However, as outlined before, many of the e-government projects that were claimed to transform government failed and no real transformation of government did take place as the focus was only on technical solutions and provisioning of government services through digital means (Alsaeed et al. 2014; Anthopoulos et al. 2016; Bannister and Connolly 2011; Choi et al. 2016; Das Aundhe et al. 2016; Gunawong and Gao 2017; Omar et al. 2017; Sehli et al. 2016; Waller and Weerakkody 2016). As such, there is a need to understand thoroughly how transformation of government as a construct affects trust and confidence in government in the presence of factors such as government performance and citizen satisfaction. Knowledge about this relationship between transformation of government, government performance, citizen satisfaction and trust and confidence in government could provide some way forward to arrest the decline in citizens' trust in government. For the purpose of this research, Transformation of Government is defined as fundamental changes to the way core functions of government are performed to achieve noticeable gains in performance and efficiency. As for factors influencing transformation of government, expectations on the ability of e-government to transform governments has motivated citizens and showed promise in reversing the trend of declining trust in governments. Notwithstanding, alongside e-government there are other factors such as technology adopted by the government organizations, citizens' expectations, transparency and accountability that need to be considered as well as to know their influence on the transformation of government which could lead to the reversal of declining trust in governments.

From reviewing the literature, it is clear that there is a need to further investigate the decline in trust and confidence of people in their governments. Moreover, there is a lack of studies that investigate the relationship and influence of transformation of government on citizens' trust and confidence in government. This research posits that this is the main gap in the literature that needs to be bridged. To do so, it is important to define the factors influencing transformation of government and the influence of each on transformation. This argument provided the rationale and motivations for conducting this research.

Like in Western Europe, many other regions of the world, including countries in the Middle East, North Africa, East Asia and Latin America have witnessed failed e-government efforts and investments towards digital enable transformation efforts in government (World Employment and Social Outlook Trends 2015, 2016, 2017). The GCC region, part of the Middle East region, have an advanced e-government platform and systems that have been recognised by the United Nations as shown in their E-Government Survey Reports released in 2012, 2014 and 2016. This advancement could not have been achieved by the GCC countries without investing heavily and commitment from the leaders towards achieving an impactful transformation in their governments' efforts to deliver improved services. Yet, in line with the rest of the world, electronic participation in GCC countries is considered as a main challenge (United Nations E-Government Survey Reports 2012, 2014, 2016). Moreover, the World Employment and Social Outlook Trends (2015, 2016, 2017) illustrate that Middle East countries faced a tremendous decline in citizens' trust and confidence in government. Some scholars such as Al-Shafi and Weerakkody (2008) and AlSobhi et al. (2010) have highlighted that electronic participation in GCC countries is a major challenge. They posit that citizens' trust and confidence in their government may play a key role in this phenomenon. Such decline is alarming for the GCC region and it is hard to find a comprehensive study conducted in any of the GCC countries that investigated the decline of citizens' trust and confidence in government and the role that transformation of government may play in tackling this decline.

This lack of evidence motivated this study and offered the right setting to conduct research making the geographic context interesting and new to explore. In this respect, Bahrain as part of the GCC countries, has been selected for conducting the research. The size of Bahrain (i.e. being the smallest country in the GCC region), level of e-government development (i.e. being the most advanced country in e-government development and implementation as per the United National Surveys 2012, 2014 and 2016), commitment from its government for e-government systems (i.e. around $106 million, has been allocated for digital government initiatives in Bahrain since the inception of the e-government initiative in 2007), and the challenges faced by Bahrain in the area of e-participation (United Nations E-Government Survey 2014, 2016) offer further justification for the study. These justifications place the GCC in general and Bahrain in particular as an attractive country for conducting this study. The findings of this research is also relevant for the rest of the GCC countries since all are advanced and mature in the implementation of the e-government and share the same culture. Countries who have just started or are in the process of commencing projects related to digital enabled transformation of governments can benefit in particular from the outcomes of this research.

Keeping the above aspects in view, this research aims to answer three research questions: (1) what factors influence transformation of government, (2) how these factors influence transformation, and (3) how transformation of government can be related to trust and confidence in citizens. The answers to these research questions are expected to enable the researcher to achieve the following aim and objectives.

1.4 Research Aim and Objectives

The aim of this research is to investigate how digital transformation of government influences citizens' trust and confidence in government.

The above aim is achieved by pursuing the following objectives:

1. Examining the current literature on factors influencing transformation of government and analysing the relationship that exists between those factors and 'transformation of government'.
2. In a similar vein, studying the extant literature and reviewing the theories and models that could be used to understand the concepts of transformation of government and citizens' trust and confidence, as well as examining the relationship between the two concepts through proposing a conceptual model and hypotheses.
3. Defining the methodological framework for conducting empirical research to test the proposed hypotheses.
4. Analysing the empirical findings and highlighting the key relationships between the different constructs proposed in the conceptual model.
5. Discussing the key findings in relation to the literature, outlining the main theoretical and practical implications of the study and offering suggestions for future research.

1.5 Significance of the Research

This research and its outcomes synthesise and enrich the information system literature and in particular the areas of *transformation of government* and *citizens' trust and confidence in government*. The main contribution of the research is that this research is considered as a novel contribution to the body of knowledge due to the fact that it is the first of its type, as per the researches' knowledge, that investigated from citizens' perspective the relationship between transformation and citizens' trust and confidence in government. Outcomes of this research will help in advancing the understanding of how transformation of government—through fundamental changes to the core functions and processes of government—can influence citizens' perception of government and their engagement with government.

Additionally, findings of the research show that e-government and technology are not enough for achieving a successful transformation of government and thus reversing the decline in citizens' trust and confidence in government. Other factors should be considered in this equation, which are adoption of transparency by the government in all of its functions and activities, practicing accountability and meeting citizens' expectations and demands.

The developed conceptual model is considered a novel contribution of this research. Thus, it may be used as a frame of reference for both the policy makers and researchers for better understanding the decline in citizens' trust and confidence in government as well as the role of transformation in reversing this decline. In addition to the theoretical contributions, the research outlines some implications for policy makers. For instance, it provides insights into the critical factors influencing citizens' trust and confidence in government and the effect of transformation of government on citizens' trust and confidence in government. By recognising these factors, any new efforts that are focused on transforming government functions have the opportunity to take into account their influence when implementing such change. For the research community, the conceptual model proposed in the study deviates from the norm of using technology or user centric theories, to propose a novel model based on the core concepts of e-government, which include, transformation of government, performance improvement, transparency and accountability. This is significant as researchers have for nearly two decades continued to view e-government with a techno-centric view and repeatedly used theories and models that are derived from private sector contexts, which have had limited effect on practice. By focusing on the core concepts of e-government and how they relate to and can be influenced by fundamental changes to the structure and the way government functions (through ICT enabled transformation of government), this research advances the current knowledge that has been recycled and thus been stagnant for several decades.

1.6 Research Methodology

A quantitative research methodology has been adopted based on a number of reasons as explained hereafter. This research investigates from citizens' perspectives the influence of transformation of government on citizens' trust and confidence in government, which is a phenomenon that is discussed in this research through testing current theory, validating the developed conceptual model and proposed hypotheses. As such, positivism is the adopted research philosophy within which citizens' perception are gathered to validate the proposed research model and associated constructs and hypotheses. Since the target audiences of this research are ordinary citizens of the Kingdom of Bahrain, a quantitative methodology is suitable to capture a large portion of the general citizens' perception on the proposed hypotheses. The use of a quantitative methodology in this research is in line with similar studies conducted previously in IS research (e.g. Morgeson et al. 2011; Teo et al. 2008; Tolbert and Mossberger 2006).

Within the quantitative frame, an online survey was developed and distributed randomly through different means such as email, SMS and social media applications to ordinary citizens living in the Kingdom of Bahrain for the purposes of capturing the views of a large number of ordinary citizens from different places in the Kingdom of Bahrain as well as variety of backgrounds. Following the data collection, SEM was chosen as a multivariate technique for this research to validate the fitness of the conceptual model and test the hypotheses through performing CFA and path analysis.

1.7 Research Outline

The structure of this Ph.D. thesis followed the methodology of Phillips and Pugh (2010) which includes four phases being (a) background theory, (b) focal theory, (c) data theory, and (d) novel contribution. The background theory is about the area of the problem along with the supported literature (Chap. 2). Focal theory deals with the development of the conceptual model (Chap. 3). On the other hand, data theory is related with issues such as research approach, methodology and protocol (Chap. 4). The next one is the data theory that is about the process of data collection and analysis (Chap. 5). Finally, the novel contribution is about the findings of the research (Chaps. 6 and 7). The below sections provide a summary of the seven chapters of this thesis.

Chapter 1: Introduction

This chapter presents an overview of the research and identifies the research gap, questions, aim and objectives. The chapter covers the rationale and motivations for conducting this research, significance of the research, research methodology and finally research outline.

Chapter 2: Literature Review—Background Theory

The literature review is covered in Chap. 2, which is about identification of key factors influencing transformation of government and trust and confidence in government along with supporting theories for each. Furthermore, the chapter presents and discusses different theories and models that are supporting the concepts covered in this research as well as the potential relationships between transformation of government and citizens' trust and confidence in government.

Chapter 3: Conceptual Model—Focal Theory

This chapter presents and explains the developed conceptual model as well as its foundations taking into account the factors identified during the literature phase. Further, theories that support the defined constructs and proposed hypotheses within the conceptual model are discussed.

Chapter 4: Research Methodology—Data Theory

This chapter provides an overview of the suitable methodology and the related research techniques adopted for this research. It starts with justifying the reasons for selecting positivist as a research philosophy compared to interpretive and critical research. Then, it moves to the research purpose where justifications are outlined for the selection of explanatory as a research purpose. Stages of the research process is illustrated which contains six phases.

Chapter 5: Findings—Data Theory

Chapter 5 presents the data analysis including different tests performed and findings of the CFA and path analysis. The roles of mediators in the conceptual model are clarified as well as the direct and indirect effects of all paths. SEM is chosen as a multivariate technique for this research to validate the fitness of the conceptual model and test the hypotheses. Before performing CFA and path analysis, a number of tests were conducted to prepare a clean data for the SEM, which included exploratory factor analysis, reliability and validity of the research instrument, correlation and normality of the data distribution.

Chapter 6: Discussion—Novel Contribution

Chapter 6 discusses the findings of the data analysis as well as maps the findings to the gap identified and the three questions agreed for this research. In this chapter, answers to the three research questions and results of the eight hypotheses are thoroughly discussed, justified, explained and linked to practical outcomes. The findings of this research illustrate that transformation of government has a significant positive effect on citizens' trust and confidence in their government. It is interesting to find out that e-government and technology are not sufficient for achieving a true transformed government and as such three other factors should be considered, which are, citizens' expectations, adoption of transparency and activating accountability.

Chapter 7: Conclusions—Novel Contribution

This chapter identifies a number of research contributions as well as practical implications to policy makers and practitioners. The research limitations and suggestions for future research are presented and discussed. Finally, the aim and objectives of the research are revisited.

As far as the researcher's knowledge, this research is first of its type that investigates from citizens' perspective the relationship between 'transformation' and 'citizens' trust and confidence in government'. Therefore, this research is considered as a novel contribution to the body of knowledge.

1.8 Summary

This chapter provided an overview of the research including the rationale and motivations for commencing the research, presented several key literatures to support the research gap, presented research questions and reasons for selecting Bahrain for conducting this research and outlined the aim and objectives of the study. The key gap found in the literature is the lack of knowledge on how transformation of government is influencing citizens' trust and confidence in government. Therefore, this research aims to investigate the relationship between transformation of government and citizens' trust and confidence in government. The research posits that, if this relationship is understood, the declining citizens' trust and confidence in government can be tackled through focused efforts to transform government with performance, transparency and accountability in mind.

This research and its outcomes synthesise and enrich the IS literature and in particular the areas of digital government, transformation of government and citizens' trust and confidence in government. A number of theoretical and practical contributions were illustrated, which will be expanded in the remaining chapters.

References

Alharbi A, Kang K, Sohaib O (2016) Citizens engagement in e-participation on egovernment websites through swat model: a case of Saudi Arabia

Alsaeed A, Adams C, Boakes R (2014) Challenges to the successful implementation of e-government initiatives in Middle-East Arabic Countries and Syria: literature review. In: tGov workshop, vol 14

Al-Shafi S, Weerakkody V (2008) The use of wireless internet parks to facilitate adoption and diffusion of e-government services: an empirical study in Qatar. In: AMCIS 2008 Proceedings, p 322

Al-Shboul M, Rababah O, Ghnemat R, Al-Saqqa S (2014) Challenges and factors affecting the implementation of e-government in Jordan. J Softw Eng Appl 7(13):1111

Al-Sobhi F, Weerakkody V, Kamal MM (2010) An exploratory study on the role of intermediaries in delivering public services in Madinah City: case of Saudi Arabia. Transforming government. People, Process and Policy 4(1):14–36

Anthopoulos L, Reddick CG, Giannakidou I, Mavridis N (2016) Why e-government projects fail? An analysis of the Healthcare.gov website. Gov Inf Quart 33(1):161–173

Bannister F, Connolly R (2011) Trust and transformational government: a proposed framework for research. Gov Inf Quart 28(2):137–147

Basu S (2004) E-government and developing countries: an overview. Int Rev Law Comput Technol 18(1):109–132

Bean C (2015) Changing citizen confidence: orientations towards Political and Social Institutions in Australia, 1983–2010. Open Polit Sci J 8(1):1–9

Bouckaert G, Van de Walle S, Kampen JK (2005) Potential for comparative public opinion research in public administration. Int Rev Admin Sci 71(2):229–240

Bovens M, Wille A (2008) Deciphering the Dutch drop: ten explanations for decreasing political trust in The Netherlands. Int Rev Admin Sci 74(2):283–305

Choi H, Park MJ, Rho JJ, Zo H (2016) Rethinking the assessment of e-government implementation in developing countries from the perspective of the design–reality gap: applications in the Indonesian e-procurement system. Telecommun Policy 40(7):644–660

Das Aundhe M, Das Aundhe M, Narasimhan R, Narasimhan R (2016) Public private partnership (PPP) outcomes in e-government–a social capital explanation. Int J Public Sector Manag 29 (7):638–658

Edwards M (2015) The trust deficit—concepts and causes of low public trust in governments. In: Committee of Experts on Public Administration, Fourteenth session, 20–24 April 2015, Item 3 of the provisional agenda

Gunawong P, Gao P (2017) Understanding e-government failure in the developing country context: a process-oriented study. Inf Technol Dev 23(1):153–178

International Labour Office (2015) World Employment and Social Outlook: Trends 2015. International Labour Organization

International Labour Office (2016) World Employment and Social Outlook: Trends 2016. International Labour Organization

International Labour Office (2017) World Employment and Social Outlook: trends 2017. International Labour Organization

Job J (2005) How is trust in government created? It begins at home, but ends in the parliament. Aust Rev Public Aff 6(1):1–23

Kim S, Kim HJ, Lee H (2009) An institutional analysis of an e-government system for anti-corruption: The case of OPEN. Gov Inf Quart 26(1):42–50

Mahmood M (2016) Enhancing citizens' trust and confidence in government through digital transformation. Int J Electron Gov Res 12(1)

Miyata M (2011) Measuring impacts of e-government support in least developed countries: a case study of the vehicle registration service in Bhutan. Inf Technol Dev 17(2):133–152

Morgeson FV (2013) Expectations, disconfirmation, and citizen satisfaction with the US federal government: testing and expanding the model. J Public Adm Res Theor 23(2):289–305

Morgeson FV, Petrescu C (2011) Do they all perform alike? An examination of perceived performance, citizen satisfaction and trust with US federal agencies. Int Rev Admin Sci 77 (3):451–479

Morgeson FV, VanAmburg D, Mithas S (2011) Misplaced trust? Exploring the structure of the e-government-citizen trust relationship. J Public Adm Res Theor 21(2):257–283

Mukhoryanova OA, Novikova IV, Rudich SB, Bogushevich EV (2016) E-Government in the Western European Countries, Asia and in the USA. Indian J Sci Technol 9(16)

Nye J (1997) In government we don't trust. Foreign Policy 108:99–111

Omar A, Weerakkody V, Sivarajah U (2017) Digitally enabled service transformation in UK public sector: a case analysis of universal credit. Int J Inf Manage 37(4):350–356

Phillips E, Pugh D (2010) How to get a PhD: a handbook for students and their supervisors. McGraw-Hill International

Reddick C, Anthopoulos L (2014) Interactions with e-government, new digital media and traditional channel choices: citizen-initiated factors. Transforming government. People, Process and Policy 8(3):398–419

Rodríguez Bolívar MP, Alcaide Muñoz L, López Hernández AM (2016) Scientometric study of the progress and development of e-government research during the period 2000–2012. Inf Technol Dev 22(1):36–74

Scharpf F (1999) Governing in Europe: effective and democratic. Oxford University Press, Oxford

Sehli H, Cooper V, Sarkar P (2016) The role of culture in developing the e-government absorptive capacity of agencies in Saudi Arabia: a conceptual model. In: PACIS 2016 Proceedings

Siddique W (2016) Critical success factors affecting e-government policy implementation in Pakistan. JeDEM-eJournal of eDemocracy and Open Government 8(1):102–126

Teo TS, Srivastava SC, Jiang L (2008) Trust and electronic government success: an empirical study. J Manag Inf Syst 25(3):99–132

Tolbert CJ, Mossberger K (2006) The effects of e-government on trust and confidence in government. Public Adm Rev 66(3):354–369

United Nations (2012) E-government survey 2012: e-government for the people. Department of Economic and Social Affairs Division for Public Administration and Development Management

United Nations (2014) E-government survey 2014: e-government for the future we want. Department of Economic and Social Affairs Division for Public Administration and Development Management

United Nations (2016) E-government survey 2016: e-government in Support of Sustainable Development. Department of Economic and Social Affairs Division for Public Administration and Development Management

Van de Walle S, Bouckaert G (2003) Public service performance and trust in government: the problem of causality. Int J Public Adm 26(8–9):891–913

Van de Walle S, Van Roosbroek S, Bouckaert G (2008) Trust in the public sector: is there any evidence for a long-term decline? Int Rev Admin Sci 74(1):47–64

Waller P, Weerakkody V (2016) Digital government: overcoming the systemic failure of transformation. In: Working Paper 2, Brunel University, London

Weerakkody V, Janssen M, Dwivedi Y (eds) (2009) Handbook of research on ICT enabled transformational government: a global perspective. Inf Sci Ref, Hershey, PA

Welch EW, Hinnant CC, Moon MJ (2005) Linking citizen satisfaction with e-government and trust in government. J Public Adm Res Theor 15(3):371–391

West DM (2004) E-government and the transformation of service delivery and citizen attitudes. Public Adm Rev 64(1):15–27

Zwahr T, Finger M, Müller P (2005) More than digitisation-The transformative potential of e-governance: an exploratory case study. In: Proceedings of the 38th Annual Hawaii International Conference on System Sciences, 2005, HICSS'05. IEEE, p 127

Chapter 2
Literature Review

2.1 Introduction

Chapter 1 provides an overview of this research, in terms of identifying the rationale, research motivations, and gaps in the literature, whilst also listing the research questions, aim and objectives. In brief, there has been a decline in citizens' trust and confidence in government over the last few decades, and some work has been done to understand this decline in e-government initiatives and projects. Despite spending a lot of money, many e-government initiatives and projects did not meet the expectations and failed. This was because they largely focused on technical, service quality, usability and adoption aspects of ICT-enabled transformation projects in the government, which had limited impact on practice. There exists a gap in the existing research, which calls for attaining deeper insights into the decline of citizens' trust and confidence in government, and the influence of digital transformation of the government on it. In this chapter, a comprehensive review of the normative literature on citizens' trust and confidence in government, transformation of government, e-government and related factors, is conducted to delineate the key issues and themes discussed in the literature relating to this study.

Literature shows that most countries are facing a challenge in the area of public trust and confidence in governments (Edwards 2015; World Employment and Social Outlook Trends 2015, 2016, 2017). A key study by the OECD confirms that public trust and confidence in governments has continued to decline over the last few decades in OECD countries (Edwards 2015). Other studies show that a similar phenomenon could be witnessed in many other regions of the world, including countries in the Middle East, North Africa, East Asia and Latin America (World Employment and Social Outlook Trends 2015, 2016, 2017). For example, Fig. 2.1 shows the results of a survey conducted by ILO with regard to the extent of confidence people have in their national governments across several countries.

M. Mahmood, *Does Digital Transformation of Government Lead to Enhanced Citizens' Trust and Confidence in Government?*, Springer Theses,
https://doi.org/10.1007/978-3-030-01759-0_2

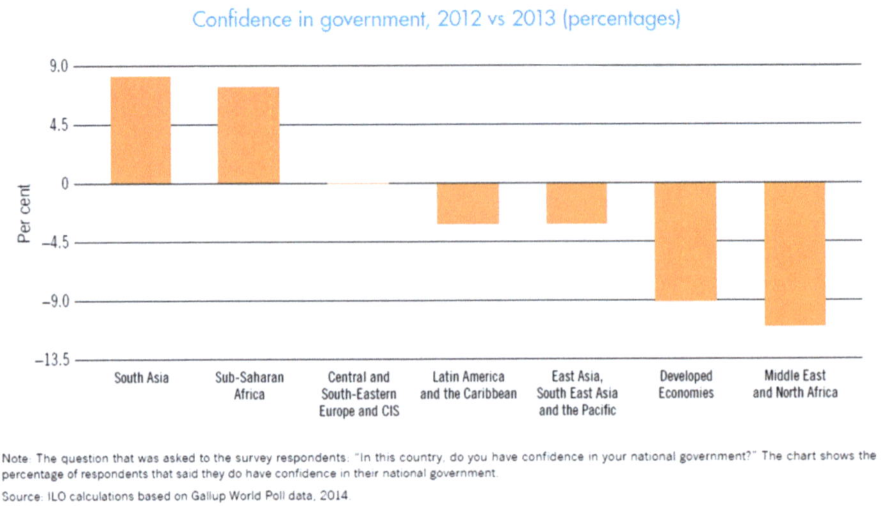

Fig. 2.1 Confidence in government. *Source* Adopted from World Employment and Social Outlook Trends 2015

Although this ILO study was released in 2015, Fig. 2.1 is representing results for 2012/13. The other ILO reports that were released in 2016 and 2017 did not include such figures.

As can be seen from Fig. 2.1, some countries in south Asia and Sub-Saharan Africa have been successful in maintaining people's trust and confidence in their governments. Despite isolated instances of certain countries where citizens continue to trust their governments, there is a broad consensus amongst researchers about the growing trust deficit and decline in people's confidence in governments (Bovens and Wille 2008; Job 2005; Nye 1997; Scharpf 1999). The reasons for this remain unclear, and the issue is being widely investigated in anticipation of solutions that can arrest such a decline.

Although literature shows some investigations (Bannister and Connolly 2011; Hong 2013; Morgeson et al. 2011; Myeong et al. 2014; Teo et al. 2008; Tolbert and Mossberger 2006; Welch et al. 2005; West 2004) have been carried out to understand the decline in trust and confidence in governments, more investigation is to be conducted to gain a deeper insight into this phenomenon. Outcomes from the current efforts are not generalizable, and in many instances are highly focused on a particular context. For instance, some studies investigate certain components of citizen experience in e-government in isolation, which does not take into account the inherent complexities and the possible influence of many potential relationships amongst factors that contribute to citizen experience (Morgeson et al. 2011). In addition, there is a lack of agreement on a common set of factors that contribute to the decline in trust and confidence of people in their governments. For instance, one factor that has been identified as a cause is the diminished performance of governments (Bean 2015; Bouckaert et al. 2005; Morgeson et al. 2011; Morgeson and Petrescu 2011; Orren 1997; Peters 1999; Van de Walle and Bouckaert 2003;

Van de Walle et al. 2008), whereas another factor identified as a cause of this decline is the rising inequality amongst the population (World Employment and Social Outlook Trends 2015, 2016, 2017). Other factors mentioned in the literature are pointed out in Table 2.2 of this chapter. Morgeson et al. (2011) argues that many studies have not produced conclusive evidence on how to handle the decline in trust and confidence in governments. There essentially is a need for further investigation into this phenomenon. Therefore, the next sections will present an extensive review of the literature on the twin concept of trust and confidence, alongside e-government, technology, transparency, accountability, citizen expectations and transformation of government, government performance and citizen satisfaction. Based on this review, this chapter will identify a clear gap that needs to be addressed to fulfil the aforementioned problem.

Middle Eastern countries are facing a rapid decline in citizen trust (−11%), which is alarming for GCC countries, overall (Fig. 2.1). The present research will be carried out in the Kingdom of Bahrain to expand on the situation in this region. This chapter is structured as follows. Section 2.2 is about the research context and justifies the choice of Bahrain for conducting this research. Section 2.3 discusses citizens' trust and confidence in government, alongside identification of the relationship between confidence and trust with applicable theories. Transformation of government and a theory supporting it is covered in Sect. 2.4. As for Sect. 2.5, it discusses e-government and its relationship with citizens' trust and confidence in government and transformation of government. Similarly, Sects. 2.6, 2.7, 2.8 and 2.9 discuss technology, citizen expectations, transparency, accountability, and their relationships with citizens' trust and confidence in government and transformation of government. Section 2.10 presents theories supporting the factors, which are expected to influence transformation of government. Performance of government and its relationship with citizens' trust and confidence in government and transformation of government is covered in Sect. 2.11. Section 2.12 discusses satisfaction and its relationship with citizens' trust and confidence in government and transformation of government. The theory supporting performance of government and citizens' satisfaction and their relationships with citizens' trust and confidence in government is highlighted in Sect. 2.13. Section 2.14 presents the gaps found in literature, with the key conclusions outlined in Sect. 2.15.

2.2 Research Context: Status of E-Government in Bahrain

Recently, e-governments in the Gulf Cooperation Countries (GCC) have achieved much in terms of deployment and implementation. Over the past few years, the governments in such countries have enhanced their services by transforming them to digital services, and making them available for citizens through e-government portals, mobile portals, e-kiosks, e-services centres *a*nd national contact centres (Al-Khouri 2012). Bahrain, in particular, has witnessed e-government transformation with various services being made available for the citizens.

Many researchers have investigated e-government in GCC countries, including Bahrain from a number of perspectives; majority of these studies have covered factors influencing adoption and diffusion of e-government services (Al-Shafi and Weerakkody 2010; Salmi and Hasnan 2016; Weerakkody et al. 2013). For instance, trust was identified as a key factor for the adoption of e-government services (Al-Khouri 2012; Al-Shafi and Weerakkody 2010; Osman et al. 2011). Additionally, culture and social influences were considered important factors by many researchers (Albusaidy and Weerakkody 2008; Al-Sobhi et al. 2010; Carter and Weerakkody 2008; Khalil 2011; Shafi and Weerakkody 2009). Rodrigues et al. (2016) suggest that confidentiality, trust, and attitude towards technology use are major factors for e-government adoption in the UAE. For Saudi Arabia, confidentiality, privacy, and security are identified as important factors to be considered by the government for run successful e-government services (Yamin and Mattar 2016).

In addition to these factors, responsiveness, efficiency and reliability were considered critical for determining the quality of e-governments (Sharma et al. 2015). As indicated, a high percentage of the available studies focused on factors influencing adoption of e-government services, in general. Moreover, no study conducted in the GCC countries has investigated trust as a dependent factor, or explored the impact of transformation of governments on citizens' trust and confidence in those governments. Thus, this research is motivated to focus on transformation of government, and to investigate whether such transformation influences citizens' trust and confidence in the government.

As per the international community and specifically, the E-Government Development Index (EGDI) of the United Nations (UN), efforts of GCC countries towards e-government have been recognized (United Nations E-Government Survey 2012, 2014, 2016). The EGDI is an established Index that consists of three sub-indicators: Global Government Index, Online Service Index and E-Participation Index (United Nations E-Government Survey 2012, 2014, 2016). To measure the status of these three sub-indicators, the UN conducts a survey every two years. The recent survey results were published in the year 2016, (Table 2.1). The table below is indicative of EGDI rankings for the GCC countries. It is clear

Table 2.1 GCC ranking globally

	E-Government Development Index (EGDI) ranking			
	2005	2012	2014	2016
Bahrain	53	36	18	24
KSA	80	41	36	44
Qatar	62	48	44	48
UAE	42	28	32	29
Oman	112	64	48	66
Kuwait	75	63	49	40

Adopted from United Nations e-government surveys

that the numbers have experienced considerable fluctuation since 2005, which indicates a lack of sustainability in the e-government services. Furthermore, the results indicate a need for further investigation of this issue.

The UN Surveys of 2014 and 2016 showed that the electronic participation levels were not as expected in both developed and developing countries. The electronic participation levels in GCC countries represent key challenges that may be related to citizens' trust in their governments (Al-Shafi and Weerakkody 2008; Al-Sobhi et al. 2010). These factors make the developing countries an interesting area to investigate, compared to the developed countries. Therefore, this area will be considered for investigation in this research, with particular attention focused on Bahrain. According to Mahmood and Weerakkody (2014), Bahrain as a developing country has been committed to various ICT initiatives to provide a higher level of services to the public. This commitment has resulted in taking digital services to an advanced stage of e-government implementation. However, as mentioned, the governments are still facing challenges with the level of citizen engagement in government services.

E-government initiatives in Bahrain have resulted in a transformed government, improved interaction and engagement with government, better quality of services, cost savings, socio-economic benefits and satisfied citizens (Mahmood and Weerakkody 2014; United Nations E-Government Survey 2014). In summary, over 300 e-government services are provided to citizens through different means as pointed out above (iGA, June 2016). With respect to the e-government portal, there were 782,221 visits in total, with the services being used by 468,892 people, and 59,658 transactions being made. A total of BD 3,355,021 was collected in 2016 (iGA, June 2016). As for mobile services, 754,201 people used them, 4379 transactions were made, and BD 231,306 was collected. The kiosk devices were used by 4761 people, 744 transactions were made and BD 6871 was collected (iGA, June 2016). These statistics show that despite being the smallest of all GCC countries, e-government in Bahrain is the most advanced in the region, which is also confirmed by the UN Surveys. These advancements would not be accomplished without the full support from the government. Around $106 million has been allocated for digital government initiatives in Bahrain, since the inception of the e-government initiative in 2007 (iGA, 2017). However, like with other GCC countries, e-participation remains a key challenge for Bahrain (United Nations E-Government Survey 2014, 2016), and it is to do with citizens' trust and confidence in the government (Mahmood and Weerakkody 2014).

Literature lacks studies conducted in Bahrain for investigating the relationship between transformation of government and citizens' trust in the government. This makes Bahrain a good choice for investigating the influence of transformation of government on citizens' trust and confidence in the government. It will also help in identifying the key factors that contribute to the successful transformation of a government. The following section will provide an overview of trust and confidence in government, and its relationship with other factors from the existing literature, which will form the basis of this research.

2.3 Trust and Confidence in Government

The concept of trust is described as unclear, deceptive, abstract, shared, multi-faceted, multidisciplinary and complex (Edwards 2015). Some argue that the meaning of trust and its content can be different in different nations and cultural backgrounds (Edwards 2015). It also argued that the meaning of trust could change over time (Edwards 2015). For this research, trust in general indicates public trust. According to the World Bank (2010), trust has many definitions. Broadly, it is used to denote citizens' assessment of a government's privilege to execute its decisions, laws and regulations, alongside the probability that the government will ensure the delivery of its commitments to its people (World Bank 2010). While many definitions of public trust exist in the literature (Edwards 2015), it can be broadly interpreted as citizens' attitude towards the government and its employees. The key question for this research revolves around the decline of public trust in government and its employees, a phenomenon that is raising concerns for the governments, its employees, and the researchers (Carter and Belanger 2005; Meijer et al. 2012; Tolbert and Mossberger 2006; Welch et al. 2005; West 2004).

This topic has attracted the attention of many researchers and is currently a serious topic of discussion in many nations, due to the important role it plays in understanding citizen behavior towards the government. Literature shows that a number of questions pertaining to trust are still an area of concern for the researchers (Bannister and Connolly 2011; Mahmood and Weerakkody 2014; Morgeson and Petrescu 2011; Morgeson et al. 2011). For instance, researchers continue to investigate why trust changes over time, what factors contribute to the decline in trust, and what factors drive change in trust in the government (Wolak and Palus 2010). While investigations continue, it is clear that there is no unique set of factors that affect public trust in government. Some of the factors that have been identified in the literature are listed in Table 2.2.

Table 2.2 Factors affecting public trust in government

#	Factors	References
1	E-Government	Morgeson et al. (2011); Tolbert and Mossberger (2006)
2	Technology	Morgeson et al. (2011); Tolbert and Mossberger (2006)
3	Accountability	Bannister and Connolly (2011); Kim et al. (2009)
4	Transparency	Bannister and Connolly (2011); Kim et al. (2009)
5	Expectation	Morgeson and Petrescu (2011); Morgeson et al. (2011)
6	Transformation of government	Bannister and Connolly (2011); Kim et al. (2009); Morgeson and Petrescu (2011)
7	Performance	Bouckaert et al. (2005); Morgeson and Petrescu (2011); Morgeson et al. (2011); Van de Walle and Bouckaert (2003); Van de Walle et al. (2008)
8	Satisfaction	Bouckaert et al. (2005); Morgeson and Petrescu (2011); Morgeson et al. (2011); Teo et al. (2008); Van de Walle and Bouckaert (2003); Van de Walle et al. (2008)

However, most of the factors identified in the extant literature need greater understanding in terms of how they influence public trust in governments. For instance, some researchers argue that citizen satisfaction is a major factor that affects public trust in government (Morgeson et al. 2011; Teo et al. 2008). Some others argue that transformation is another factor that affects citizen trust (Bannister and Connolly 2011; Kim et al. 2009). Competence, benevolence and honesty are amongst the other identified factors determining citizen trust in governments (Grimmelikhuijsen 2009). However, one important factor that seems to be repeated by researchers in determining public trust in government is the concept of e-government. Many argue that e-government has a direct bearing on the trust level of citizens in their governments (Grimmelikhuijsen 2009; Morgeson et al. 2011; Tolbert and Mossberger 2006), while some others argue that e-government indirectly influences public trust (Abu-Shanab and Al-Azzam 2012; Bélanger and Carter 2008; Carter and Bélanger 2005; Colesca 2009; Navarrete 2010; Teo et al. 2008). E-government's potential to transform governments is motivating for the citizens, and showing promise in reversing the trend of their declining trust in governments. There are other factors to be considered (see Table 2.2), so their influence on the transformation of government can be studied to reverse the declining trust in governments. The other important factor found to affect people of a nation is their confidence in their governments. There appears to be a close relationship between trust and confidence. A review of the concept of confidence was considered necessary to establish the relationship between trust and confidence.

2.3.1 Relationship Between Confidence and Trust

The concept of public confidence is considered an important feature that affects governance. Public confidence is considered critical whilst measuring the quality of governance and the extent of trust that the citizens have on governments (Mungiu-Pippidi et al. 2016). Confidence of citizens is widely related to the level of corruption in countries, with literature hinting that higher the confidence of citizens in governance, lower is the corruption level and vice versa (Mungiu-Pippidi et al. 2016). Thus, public confidence becomes an important concept that needs to be considered while discussing transformation of governments.

Prior research shows that confidence is a concept that is closely related to public trust (e.g. Mungiu-Pippidi et al. 2016; Wolak and Palus 2010). For instance, a study by Mungiu-Pippidi et al. (2016) shows that between 2008 and 2015, Europe has witnessed a fall in trust in governance due to the loss of citizens' confidence to some extent. Similar arguments are found in the American context; in their study on public confidence in the U.S. State and local governments, Wolak and Palus (2010) brought out a number of arguments posited by other authors, which indicated that trust is influenced by confidence (e.g. Uslaner 2001). However, questions are raised on whether the dynamics of changing confidence levels can be related to the decline

Table 2.3 Relationship between confidence and trust

No.	Relationship between confidence and trust	Authors
1	Trust reflects the degree of confidence and goodwill directed toward governing institutions	Lai et al. (2010)
2	Trust is the information governing institutions share with stakeholders	Gilmour et al. (2015)
3	Governance is a means to build confidence and trust	Khan (2016)
4	Consequence of governance failures could result in loss of confidence and trust	Hess and Hess (2016)
5	Trust and confidence have often been viewed as crucial elements in evaluating the performance	Fukuyama (1995); Sargeant and Lee (2002); Toppe and Kirsh (2003)
6	Social trust refers to citizens' confidence in each other as members of a community	Edwards (2015)

in citizen trust (Wolak and Palus 2010). Literature shows that a number of authors have argued that trust and confidence are inseparable concepts (see Table 2.3).

In addition to its relationship to trust, confidence is explained as a challenge for transformation of government. For instance, Al-Shboul et al. (2014) investigated the implementation of e-government in Jordan, and found that public confidence and trust act as barriers to the transformation of government; Siddique (2016) and Mahmood (2016) also support this claim. However, it is not clear from the current literature that how the dynamics of confidence and trust work, and how they change over a period of time (Wolak and Palus 2010). Therefore, it becomes important to consider confidence and trust as a single entity, due to their inseparable nature when governance is involved.

Furthermore, both performance of the government and citizen satisfaction have been identified as important constructs affecting citizens' confidence and trust (Bean 2015). There is a need to examine new determinants of government performance and citizen satisfaction that have not yet been considered in the literature; for instance, determinants of e-participation and citizen satisfaction in e-participation (Alharbi et al. 2016). This argument can be extended to government transformation as a determinant of government performance and citizen satisfaction. There is also a need to understand how transformation of government as a construct affects trust and confidence in government, in the presence of factors such as government performance and citizen satisfaction. This research problem is applicable to Bahrain. Knowledge about the relationship between transformation of government, government performance, citizen satisfaction and trust and confidence in government could offer some solutions capable of arresting the decline of citizen trust in governments.

2.3.2 Theories on Citizen Trust and Confidence

This section will provide a grounded theory for trust and confidence to support the conceptual model. From the current literature, two theories were found supportive of trust and confidence, which are micro-performance theory (Van de Walle and Bouckaert 2003) and exit-voice theory (Fornell et al. 1996; Hirschman 1970; Morgeson et al. 2011).

This research is expanding the investigation conducted by Morgeson et al. (2011) to further investigate the concept of trust and confidence in government through a transformed government. The conceptual model proposed by Morgeson et al. (2011) was based on theories related to the marketing discipline that focused on formation of consumer attitude (Bearden and Teal 1983; Cadotte et al. 1987; Churchill and Surprenant 1982; Fornell et al. 1996; Oliver 1980; Parasuraman et al. 1991). Many studies (Donnelly et al. 1995; Fornell et al. 1996, 2009a, b; James 2009; Poister and Henry 1994; Van Ryzin et al. 2004) have adapted, applied and used these theories and models in the government for specifically exploring citizens' attitude towards services provided by the government.

This research will focus on the core theory identified by Morgeson et al. (2011), which is the exit-voice theory (Hirschman 1970). It states that when customers are satisfied, there are fewer complaints and loyalty is increased. Otherwise, customers have the option to exit (move to a competitor) or voice their complaints. The model developed by Morgeson et al. (2011) was tested and validated to understand citizens' trust and confidence in government in an e-government and managing citizen expectations context. It can thus be used for this research to build a model that investigates the influence of transformation of government on citizens' trust and confidence, mediated by citizens' perceived performance of government and citizen satisfaction.

The second theory was the micro-performance theory that supports the relationships between performance of the government and citizens' satisfaction as well as between citizens' satisfaction and citizens' trust and confidence in government. It is very simple and straightforward, and considers trust in government as the ultimate outcome. Better performance of government results in satisfied citizens, which in turn enhances their trust in government (Van de Walle and Bouckaert 2003). A number of prior studies (Kampen et al. 2003, 2006; Van de Walle and Bouckaert 2003) have used the micro-performance theory to understand the relationship between government performance and trust, which is mediated by citizen satisfaction. Therefore, the micro-performance theory and the aforementioned studies can be considered as useful guides for investigating the relationship between transformation of government, citizen satisfaction, and citizen trust and confidence in government. In the context of this research, the transformed government has the potential to increase the number of satisfied citizens, which in turn enhances citizen trust and confidence in government.

Although the micro-performance theory supports the proposed conceptual model to some extent, it has not been used in the e-government literature or the transformation of government literature, if one can call it so. In contrast, exit-voice theory has been tested, validated and used in the e-government literature, and is therefore regarded as the dominant theory for this research to support the proposed conceptual model.

2.4 Transformation of Government

Although digital government initiatives have been introduced in most parts of the world, some of which are in their advanced stages, citizens' trust in governments still remains a concerning issue for most (Bean 2015; Edwards 2015; Morgeson et al. 2011; Teo et al. 2008; World Employment and Social Outlook Trends 2015, 2016, 2017). Moreover, many of the initiatives that have been implemented, very few have achieved real transformation of government (i.e. fundamental changes to the way core functions of government are performed to achieve noticeable gains in performance and efficiency). As such, there is a need to understand how transformation of government as a construct affects citizens' trust and confidence in government in the presence of factors such as, government performance and citizen satisfaction (Bannister and Connolly 2011; Kim et al. 2009; Morgeson et al. 2011; Morgeson and Petrescu 2011; Weerakkody et al. 2009; Welch et al. 2005). Since there is no single definition for the term transformation of government (Bannister and Connolly 2011; West 2004), it should be given proper consideration in this research. In many studies, this term refers to improvement of operational efficiency (Seifert and Chung 2009; Waller and Weerakkody 2016; Zwahr et al. 2005) and changes in process, structure, lines of authority, focus, power, and so on (Bannister and Connolly 2011; Cabinet Office 2005; Moon and Norris 2005; Waller and Weerakkody 2016). Furthermore, some researchers (Layne and Lee 2001; Lee 2007; Siau and Long 2005; Waller and Weerakkody 2016) and international organizations (European Commission 2015; United Nations 2014) have considered transformation as a stage of digital government development.

In addition, Bonham et al. (2001) previously defined the stages of transformation and pointed out that the final stage can be defined as using technology to "transform how government functions are conceived, organized and executed" (p. 6). The stages of transformation may be expressed in terms of quality, rather than being directly focused on the changes in the process and structure. Such stages can cluster the transformation. However, it does provide the actual definition of transformation, which is yet not fully understood, and requires further investigation (Bannister and Connolly 2011; West 2004). The key focus was thus technical, rather than on government's core businesses and functions, resulting in the development of means to deliver services provided by governments (Bannister and Connolly 2011; O'Neill 2009; Waller and Weerakkody 2016).

E-government has been an area of interest for IS researchers since the last two decades, which is the main reason for this technical focus on transformation of government (Waller and Weerakkody 2016). These conflicting conclusions on the definitions and role of transformation of government lead a number of researchers to define it as changing the policy instrument set chosen to implement policy (Bannister and Connolly 2011; Waller and Weerakkody 2016; Zwahr et al 2005). Researchers have argued that transformation is about changing the government functions and policies, and not about developing new websites or other innovative ways to deliver government services (Bannister and Connolly 2011; Waller and Weerakkody 2016). Here, ICT plays a major role in changing government policies, which is referred to as ICT-enabled government transformation. As it can be seen here, the focus is on changing public administration, which can be referred to real transformation of government.

Furthermore, Janssen and Shu (2008) have defined transformational government as transparent, accountable, efficient, and agile. However, they found that few governments are adapting to these elements, which makes the problem much acute. Therefore, this research is focused on the relationship between transparency, accountability, technology, citizen expectations and e-government and transformational government. In addition, Bannister and Connolly (2011) find that government transformation is described as fluid, and yet a question in the literature is left unanswered that is the relationship between transformation of government and citizens' trust and confidence in government. However, in order to be able to measure the governmental transformation, the trust of citizens is required. In line with arguments from Bannister and Connolly (2011) and Janssen and Shu (2008), citizen expectation is considered as an important element, and is thus a part of the proposed conceptual model for this research. In addition, citizen trust is required, which is supported by their expectations.

Transformation of government has been investigated towards trusted services provided to the public, rather than being focused on processes delivered through ICT only; therefore, technology and e-government play a vital role in transformation of government (Bannister and Connolly 2011). Moreover, other factors were called to be discussed along with technology and e-government. Hudson (2006) found that performance plays a role towards trust in the government, and other researchers supported this claim (Abramson 1983; Maddox and Lilie 1984; Nye et al. 1997). E-government mainly transforms government, and with the use of ICT change will lead to better performance of the government. Therefore, performance is a component that should be considered a part of the conceptual model proposed in this study.

From the above arguments, it can be noted that literature has conflicting definitions for transformation of government, which needs to be investigated further. Thus, transformation of government will also be included in the conceptual model for this research. For the purpose of this research, Transformation of Government is defined as fundamental changes to the way core functions of government are performed to achieve noticeable gains in performance and efficiency.

In the context of Bahrain, no previous studies have investigated transformation of government, or factors influencing it. The outcome of this research is expected to add to the current knowledge, whilst offering a better understanding on the concept of transformation of government, and the role of transparency, accountability, technology, citizen expectations, and e-government.

2.4.1 *Theory on Transformation of Government*

From the current literature, only one theory was found supportive to the concept of transformation of government, which is the public administration theory (Zouridis and Thaens 2003). This section will provide a grounded theory for transformation of government to support the conceptual model proposed in this research.

The public administration theory supports the relationship between transformation of government and performance; the traditional government/public administration will change and result in an ICT-enabled transformed government/public administration that integrates transparency and accountability into its work, functions and activities, and manages citizen expectations. This transformation will result in improved government services, and enhance efficiency and effectiveness of the transformed government. The public administration theory is related to this research, as it covers the main aspects of citizen expectations whilst also considering the performance aspects.

According to Zouridis and Thaens (2003), the fundamental character of public administration and the basic structure of its institutions are affected by the transformed government.

2.5 E-Government and Its Relationship with Transformation of Government, and Citizens' Trust and Confidence

Trust in government has faced a continuous decline, which has been left unresolved. Literature has investigated digital government initiatives with an objective of fulfilling this gap (Bannister and Connolly 2011; Grimmelikhuijsen 2009; Morgeson et al. 2011; Teo et al. 2008; Tolbert and Mossberger 2006). Despite many attempts, outcomes of the undertaken studies investigating the relationship between trust, government and digital government, are conflicting in nature. For instance, while some authors (Al-Shafi and Weerakkody 2008, 2010; Srivastava and Teo 2009; Tolbert and Mossberger 2006; Welch et al. 2005; West 2004) proposed that digital government enhances trust in government, the others (Grimmelikhuijsen 2009; McNeal et al. 2008; Morgreson et al. 2011; Pina et al. 2009; West 2004) stated that trust in government can only be enhanced through transparency in information and services.

According to Mahmood and Weerakkody (2014), this conflicting relationship needs to be further investigated, which is expected to better our understanding of the relationship between e-government and citizen trust. Therefore, this study will focus on the relationship between e-government and citizen trust, mediated by other factors (identified in the literature) that may have an influence on citizen trust and confidence in government.

West (2004) stated that e-government refers to the delivery of government-related information and services made available to citizens through online means or other digital mechanisms. E-government was adopted by many countries with an expectation of improving citizen trust and confidence. However, despite spending a high amount of money on digital government projects, the developing countries in particular still face the problem of decline in citizen trust and confidence.

Some researchers argued that the failure of such e-government projects was due to the focus on technical aspects, and not on government's core businesses and functions resulting in the development of means to deliver government services (Bannister and Connolly 2011; Gunawong and Gao 2017; Omar et al. 2017; O'Neill 2009; Waller and Weerakkody 2016). On the other hand, some researchers (Bannister and Connolly 2011; O'Neill 2009; Tolbert and Mossberger 2006; Waller and Weerakkody 2016) believe that transparency may also have a role in obtaining citizen trust and confidence in the government. However, due to the lack of investigation on the concept of transformation of government, the influence of e-government and other factors has still not been comprehensively discussed in the literature.

2.6 Technology and Its Relationship with Transformation of Government and Citizen Trust and Confidence

According to Hiller and Belanger (2001), adopting technology through IT services throughout government operations will help government fulfil their responsibility towards citizen in a more effective and transparent manner. Thus, technology plays a role in supporting citizen trust and confidence in government as it provides transparent service. This still leaves a gap unaddressed, which is the relationship between technology and citizen trust and confidence in government, without considering other factors that may also have an influence on trust and confidence.

Some researchers have argued that technology in government refers to IT and its impact on business management (Al Rub 2006). Other researchers (Bannister and Connolly 2011; Waller and Weerakkody 2016) have highlighted the need for technology in changing government policies by being a part of the policy design process. Thus, it can be argued that changing government policies could also be considered as transformation of government. Therefore, there is a need to investigate the relationship between technology, e-government and transparency, which may lead to citizen trust and confidence. Technology is expected to work closely with transparency and e-government, resulting in transformation of the government that is further expected to enhance citizen trust and confidence in government.

2.7 Citizen Expectations and Their Relationship with Transformation of Government and Citizen Trust and Confidence in Government

According to Parasuraman et al. (1988), citizen expectation is defined as customers' perceptions of what a service should offer. In case of trust and confidence, citizens have a set of expectations in terms of what the government should offer. In support of this argument, Nam (2012) states that public expectation is the most determining factor that facilitates decline in public's trust of government, and the same becomes applicable to Bahrain. Morgeson et al. (2011) investigated the relationship between citizen expectation, satisfaction, citizen trust and confidence in the agency and Wessington. They concluded that e-government does not lead to higher citizen expectations; however, there was a significant relationship between citizen expectation and confidence with the agency. Therefore, citizen expectation is also an element that should be considered in investigating the factors that influence trust and confidence in government.

As mentioned previously, there are hardly any studies that have considered the relationship between transformation of government (Bannister and Connolly 2011) and trust and confidence in government, mediated by other influential factors highlighted in the literature on e-government, technology, transparency and accountability. Therefore, this study will investigate citizen expectation that is expected to work with e-government, technology, transparency and accountability towards transformation of government, which in turn is expected to lead to citizen trust and confidence in government.

2.8 Transparency and Its Relationship with Transformation of Government and Citizen Trust and Confidence in Government

According to Chen et al. (2003), transparency is defined as the ability of outsiders to assess the true position of a company, which is in line with arguments in literature (Bannister and Connolly 2011; O'Neill 2009; Tolbert and Mossberger 2006; Waller and Weerakkody 2016). Transparency could be a key element for enhancing citizen trust and confidence in government. Transparency is expected to work closely with e-government (Garcia-Murillo 2013; Mahmood and Weerakkody 2014) and technology (Garcia-Murillo 2013; Chen et al. 2003) leading to transformation of government.

However, as argued by some authors (O'Neill 2009; Tolbert and Mossberger 2006), transparency is key for enhancing citizen trust and confidence in government. Therefore, transparency cannot be neglected or investigated separately. This argument is also supported in literature (Chen et al. 2003; Song and Lee 2013; Welch et al. 2005), which highlights that transparency is a core element for achieving transformation of government. Technology plays a major role in increasing transparency, which in turn enhances the performance of government and improves citizen trust and confidence.

2.9 Accountability and Its Relationship with Transformation of Government and Citizen Trust and Confidence in Government

Accountability goes along with transparency and they are both considered as key elements for transformation of government (Amaliah et al. 2015; Bannister and Connolly 2011; Kim et al. 2009). On the other hand, Chen et al. (2003) defines accountability as the accountability of management to the stakeholders. In this regard, some authors (Bannister and Connolly 2011; Kim et al. 2009; Norquist 2007) argued that accountability and transparency could influence the transformation of government. Therefore, accountability will be investigated as part of this study, which is expected to work with e-government, technology and transparency towards transformation of government.

2.10 Theories Supporting Factors Predicted to Influence Transformation of Government

For the aforementioned factors chosen for this study, grounded theories previously used in research by various studies have been listed in Table 2.4.

Table 2.4 Theories supporting factors predicted to work with transformation of government

Theory	Construct
Public administration theory (Zouridis and Thaens 2003)	EGOV TECH TRANSPY ACOUNT
Institutional theory (Bekkers and Meijer 2012; Kim et al. 2009; Luna-Reyes and Gil-García 2011; Pina et al. 2009; Weerakkody et al. 2016)	EGOV TECH TRANSPY ACOUNT
Structuration Theory (Orlikowski 1992, 2000; Orlikowski et al. 1995; Meijer et al. 2012)	EGOV TECH
User adoption theories (example Technology Acceptance Model, TAM; Diffusion of Innovation, DOI) (see Gilbert and Balestrini 2004)	EGOV TECH
Agent-principal theory (Kim et al. 2009)	TRANSPY ACOUNT
Stakeholder theory (Chan et al. 2003; Pardo and Scholl 2002; Scholl 2001; Tennert and Schroeder 1999)	EXPEC

2.10.1 Theories Supporting E-Government and Technology

The first theory is the public administration theory. E-government initiatives result in transforming the government and governance to e-government and e-governance. As such, e-government redefines key parts of public administration as operating core, implementation of public policy and democratic supervision. Here, the traditional processes are transformed into information-based processes (Zouridis and Thaens 2003). As for technology and transformation of government, e-government initiatives require different government entities to use ICT technologies including hardware and software. Additionally, ICT can be used by government entities for other purposes as well, such as development of new policies, supporting citizens and strategic processes, and so on. These ICT initiatives will contribute to transforming government to be an ICT-enabled transformed government (Zouridis and Thaens 2003).

The second theory is the structuration theory that backs up the use of technologies by different government entities. This includes technologies needed for e-government initiatives as well as for their own purposes, and both would result in institutional transformation (Meijer et al. 2012). The third theory is related to user adoption. As pointed out above, introduction of technologies can result in transforming the way government manages its functions, and delivers its services to the citizens. Therefore, it can be considered an institutional transformation. However, for a successful ICT-enabled transformation of government, adoption of government services by citizens should be clear and visible. User adoption theories, for example, Technology Acceptance Model (TAM) and Diffusion of Innovation (DOI) (Gilbert and Balestrini 2004) would assist in studying the adoption of government services by the citizens.

The last theory is the institutional theory that has been referred by many researchers (Bekkers and Meijer 2012; Kim et al. 2009; Luna-Reyes and Gil-García 2011; Pina et al. 2009; Weerakkody et al. 2016) to explain and understand the ICT-enabled government. ICT included in e-government is considered a proper institution, taking into account its relationships with the surrounding environment, organizational aspects, stakeholders, communications with other government agencies, interaction with citizens and socio-economic impact on the country, in general, and the government, in particular. As such, the institutional theory along with its three forces—coercive, mimetic and normative forces, would fit the context of this research. The applicability of institutional theory comes from a number of perspectives. The main one is related to the implementation of ICT in e-government, and issues surrounding its implementation (Bekkers and Meijer 2012; Kim et al. 2009; Luna-Reyes and Gil-García 2011; Pina et al. 2009; Weerakkody et al. 2016). In this context, institutional theory is often used along with other theories such as Diffusion of Innovations Theory (Pina et al. 2009). Furthermore, the Technology enactment framework of the institutional theory has been used along with dynamic simulation, particularly, system dynamics (Luna-Reyes and Gil-García 2011).

2.10.2 Theories Supporting Transparency and Accountability

The first theory here is the public administration theory. In a transformed government, adoption of transparency supported by ICT would result in making government-related information accessible by all stakeholders, including general citizens. This by itself changes the way public administration works, acts and interacts, and how the citizens are given the freedom to appeal and escalate, if needed. The second theory is the institutional theory. ICT-enabled transformed government results in enhancing government's transparency and accountability, which in turn affects the organizational aspect and institutional arrangements, as well as the way government institutions work and interact with their stakeholders, including citizens (Kim et al. 2009; Weerakkody et al. 2016).

The third theory is the agent-principle theory. Here, Kim et al. (2009) referred agent to government and principle to citizens. This is a kind of relationship where the principle (citizens) monitors and the agent (government) performs and reports on the progress supported by evidence (Kim et al. 2009). The same principle applies to transformed government, which adopts transparency through, for example, making the necessary information related to all services, processes and procedures, available to the citizens. Additionally, the agent (government) can share different reports such as performance reports, KPIs achieved and cases dealt with. Accountability of government comes by default into the picture, when such details are made available to citizens.

2.10.3 Theory Supporting Citizen Expectations

The stakeholder theory states that, if an organization manages effectively its relationships with its stakeholders, it will perform well; otherwise, the performance will be lower (Freeman 2010). The relationship here refers to interaction with stakeholders, involvement of stakeholders in the implementation and managing stakeholders' expectations. In the context of this research, citizen expectations of a truly transformed government should be managed, and this can be performed by introducing proper communication channels and introduction of a consultation process on all aspects of government functions, activities and services (Scott et al. 2004).

2.11 Performance of Government and Its Relationship with Transformation of Government and Citizen Trust and Confidence

Digital government or e-government was used by the government with the predication that it will improve government performance, leading to citizen trust and confidence in government (Al-Shafi and Weerakkody 2008, 2010; Srivastava and

Teo 2009; Tolbert and Mossberger 2006; Welch et al. 2005; West 2004). Furthermore, Hudson (2006) highlighted that performance plays a vital role towards trust in the government, which was also supported by other researchers (Abramson 1983; Maddox and Lilie 1984; Nye et al. 1997).

The literature contains studies related to government performance and factors that may influence citizen trust and confidence, but the studies do not focus on the relationship between transformation of government and citizen trust and confidence (Bannister and Connolly 2011; Kim et al. 2009; Waller and Weerakkody 2016; West 2004). A factor contributing to the decline is citizen expectations from the government, which is once again related to the nature of services provided by the government (Orren 1997; Peters 1999). Performance is the organization's potential to make use of its own resources in an effective and efficient manner (Hameed and Al-Shawabkha 2013). To a certain extent, this argument can be associated with the transformation of government, as it leads to the use of the same resources. Citizens perceive performance as a determinant of satisfaction and trust (Morgeson and Petrescu 2011).

Therefore, the performance of an organization is based on their successful operation that affects the satisfaction of all stakeholders, including citizens (Kim et al. 2009; Morgeson et al. 2011; Tolbert and Mossberger 2006; Welch et al. 2005; West 2004). This study will thus investigate government performance that is expected to work with transformation of government and citizens' satisfaction, which in turn is expected to lead to citizens' trust and confidence in government.

2.12 Citizen Satisfaction and Its Relationship with Transformation of Government and Citizen Trust and Confidence

Citizen Satisfaction is defined as 'the sum total of a citizen's sense of fulfilment with his or her experience' (Morgeson et al. 2011). As mentioned above, citizens' expectations plays a vital role in their trust and confidence in government, as the stakeholders, who are the citizens, have specific expectations from the government (Orren 1997; Peters 1999). Some researchers argue that citizens' satisfaction is a major factor that affects public trust in government (Bean 2015; Morgeson et al. 2011; Morgeson and Petrescu 2011; Teo et al. 2008). There is a clear relationship between citizen satisfaction and citizen expectations (Morgeson et al. 2011; Morgeson and Petrescu 2011).

Two studies conducted by (Morgeson et al. 2011; Morgeson and Petrescu 2011) to test the relationship between citizens' expectation and citizens' satisfaction leading to citizens' satisfaction with the government.

This research proposes to investigate the relationship between citizens' expectation and transformation of government, leading to citizens' satisfaction and citizens' trust and confidence in government. This is supported by arguments by researchers (Bannister and Connolly 2011; Janssen and Shu 2008), who highlight that citizens' expectations are considered an important element in the formula of transformation of government.

2.13 Theory Supporting Performance of Government and Citizen Satisfaction and Their Relationship with Citizens Trust and Confidence in Government

From the current literature, only one theory was found supportive of performance of government and citizens' satisfaction, which is micro-performance theory (Kampen et al. 2003, 2006; Van de Walle and Bouckaert 2003).

The micro-performance theory supports the relationships between performance of the government and citizens' satisfaction as well as citizens' satisfaction and citizens' trust and confidence in government. It is very simple and straightforward, and considers trust in government as the ultimate outcome. Better performance of government results in satisfied citizens, which in turn enhances trust in government (Van de Walle and Bouckaert 2003). Many studies (Kampen et al. 2003, 2006; Van de Walle and Bouckaert 2003) have used the micro-performance theory to understand the relationship between performance of government and trust in government, mediated by citizens' satisfaction. As such, the theory and these studies can be considered as useful guides in investigating the relationships between transformation of government, citizens' satisfaction and citizens' trust and confidence in government. For this research, transformed government has the potential to increase the number of satisfied citizens, which in turn, will enhance citizens' trust and confidence in government.

2.14 Gap Found in Literature

From the undertaken literature review in this chapter, it is noted that there is no clear definition of 'transformation of government' till date, which does not provide enough knowledge on the relationship between transformation of government and citizens' trust and confidence in government. Despite the few studies conducted to investigate the problem of citizens' trust and confidence in government, there is hardly any research studying the transformation of government as part of a conceptual model. Other researchers have identified various factors such as, citizen satisfaction, performance of government, e-government, technology, transparency and accountability. There is however, no comprehensive study that integrates these factors into one conceptual model and measures how they work together towards the transformation of government, leading to citizens' trust and confidence in government.

Therefore, this research aims to investigate the relationship of e-government, technology, transparency, expectations, and accountability on transformation of government. This research will also investigate the relationship between transformation of government and citizens' trust and confidence in government, mediated by performance of government and citizens' satisfaction.

2.15 Summary

This chapter provides an extensive review of the literature, and is focused on the available models previously employed by the researchers in the area of citizens' trust and confidence in government. The literature review provides a summary of all components and associated theories that will be a part of the conceptual model for this research. The following chapter will present the proposed conceptual model and the hypotheses drawn in line with the existing literature to support the investigation being undertaken by this research.

References

Abramson P (1983) Political attitudes in America. Freeman, San Francisco

Abu-Shanab E, Al-Azzam A (2012) Trust dimensions and the adoption of e-government in Jordan. International Journal of Information Communication Technologies and Human Development (IJICTHD) 4(1):39–51

Al Rub S (2006) The impact of information technology on business performance management (The study of the Affairs Agency of Sudanese working abroad for the period (2000–2005). Master's thesis, University of Science and Technology, Omdurman

Albusaidy M, Weerakkody V (2008) Factors influencing e-government implementation progress in Oman: a discussion. In: Proceedings of the 2008 European and Mediterranean conference on information systems

Alharbi A, Kang K, Sohaib O (2016) Citizens engagement in e-participation on egovernment websites through swat model: a case of Saudi Arabia

Al-Khouri AM (2012) eGovernment strategies the case of the United Arab Emirates (UAE). Eur J ePractice 17:126–150

Al-Shafi S, Weerakkody V (2008) The use of wireless internet parks to facilitate adoption and diffusion of e-government services: an empirical study in Qatar. In: AMCIS 2008 proceedings, p 322

Al-Shafi S, Weerakkody V (2010) Factors affecting e-government adoption in the state of Qatar. In: Proceedings of the European and Mediterranean conference on information systems, Abu Dhabi, 12–13 Apr 2010

Al-Shboul M, Rababah O, Ghnemat R, Al-Saqqa S (2014) Challenges and factors affecting the implementation of e-government in Jordan. J Soft Eng Appl 7(13):1111

Al-Sobhi F, Weerakkody V, Kamal MM (2010) An exploratory study on the role of intermediaries in delivering public services in Madinah City: case of Saudi Arabia. Transforming Government. People, Process and Policy 4(1):14–36

Amaliah Said I, Iaafar NH, Atan R (2015) Assessing accountability in government linked companies: an empirical evidence. Int Bus Manage 9(4):460–469

Bannister F, Connolly R (2011) Trust and transformational government: a proposed framework for research. Gov Inf Quart 28(2):137–147

Bean C (2015) Changing citizen confidence: orientations towards political and social institutions in Australia, 1983–2010. Open Polit Sci J 8(1):1–9

Bearden WO, Teal JE (1983) Selected determinants of consumer satisfaction and complaint reports. J Mark Res 20(1):21–28

Bekkers, V., and Meijer, A. (2012) 'A Meta-Theory of E-Government', *In 34th EGPA Conference Proceedings*

Bélanger F, Carter L (2008) Trust and risk in e-government adoption. J Strateg Inf Syst 17 (2):165–176

Bonham G, Seifert J, Thorson S (2001) The transformational potential of e-Government: the role of political leadership. In 4th Pan European international relations conference, University of Kent, UK, Sep 2001

Bouckaert G, Van de Walle S, Kampen JK (2005) Potential for comparative public opinion research in public administration. Int Rev Admin Sci 71(2):229–240

Bovens M, Wille A (2008) Deciphering the Dutch drop: ten explanations for decreasing political trust in The Netherlands. Int Rev Admin Sci 74(2):283–305

Cabinet Office (2005) Transformational government. Cabinet Office, London

Cadotte ER, Woodruff RB, Jenkins RL (1987) Expectations and norms in models of consumer satisfaction. J Mark Res 24(3):305–314

Carter L, Bélanger F (2005) The utilization of e-government services: citizen trust, innovation and acceptance factors. Inf Syst J 15(1):5–25

Carter L, Weerakkody V (2008) E-government adoption: a cultural comparison. Inf Syst Front 10 (4):473–482

Chan CML, Shan-Ling P, Tan C-W (2003) Managing stakeholder relationships in an e-government project. In: Ninth Americas conference on information systems, Florida

Chen KC, Wei KC, Chen Z (2003) Disclosure, corporate governance, and the cost of equity capital: evidence from Asia's emerging markets. Retrieved from http://dx.doi.org/10.2139/ssrn.422000

Churchill GA Jr, Surprenant C (1982) An investigation into the determinants of customer satisfaction. J Mark Res 19(4):491–504

Colesca SE (2009) Understanding trust in e-government. Inzinerine Ekonomika-Engineering Economics 3(3):7–15

Donnelly M, Wisniewski M, Dalrymple J, Curry A (1995) Measuring service quality in local government: the SERVQUAL approach. Int J Public Sector Manage 8:15–20

Edwards M. (2015) The trust deficit—concepts and causes of low public trust in governments. In: Committee of Experts on Public Administration, Fourteenth session, 20–24 April 2015, Item 3 of the provisional agenda

European Commission (2015) eGovernment in the European Union 2015

Fornell C, Johnson MD, Anderson EW, Cha J, Bryant BE (1996) The American customer satisfaction index: nature, purpose and findings. J Mark 60(4):7–18

Fornell C, Mithas S, Morgeson III FV (2009a) Commentary—the economic and statistical significance of stock returns on customer satisfaction. Mark Sci 28:820–825

Fornell C, Mithas S, Morgeson III FV (2009b) The statistical significance of Portfolio returns. Int J Res Mark 26:162–163

Freeman RE (2010) Strategic management: a stakeholder approach. Cambridge University Press

Fukuyama F (1995) Trust: the social virtues and the creation of prosperity. Free Press, New York

Garcia-Murillo M (2013) Does a government web presence reduce perceptions of corruption? Inf Technol Dev 19(2):151–175

Gilbert D, Balestrini P (2004) Barriers and benefits in the adoption of e-government. Int J Public Sect Manage 17(4):286–301

Gilmour P, Coffey B, O'Toole K (2015) Trust and knowledge exchange in coastal settings. Aust J Marit Ocean Aff 7(1):66–74

Grimmelikhuijsen S (2009) Do transparent government agencies strengthen trust? Inf Polity 14 (3):173–186
Gunawong P, Gao P (2017) Understanding e-government failure in the developing country context: a process-oriented study. Inf Technol Dev 23(1):153–178
Hameed S, Al-Shawabkah A (2013) Role of e-government in improving organizational performance in the civil status and passports department of Jordan. Dev Country Stud 3 (5):50–64
Hess AM, Hess MF (2016) The consequences of governance failure for innovation. In: Working paper. Washington and Lee University
Hiller JS, Belanger F (2001) Privacy strategies for electronic government. E-government series. The PricewaterhouseCoopers Endowment for the Business of Government. Available at http://www.businessofgovernment.org/pdfs/HillerReport.pdf
Hirschman AO (1970) Exit, voice, and loyalty: responses to decline in firms, organizations, and states, vol 25. Harvard University Press
Hong H (2013) Government websites and social media's influence on government-public relationships. Public Relat Rev 39(4):346–356
Hudson J (2006) Institutional trust and subjective well-being across the EU. Kyklos 59(1):43–62
International Labour Office (2015) World Employment and Social Outlook: Trends 2015. International Labour Organization
International Labour Office (2016) World Employment and Social Outlook: trends 2016. International Labour Organization
International Labour Office (2017) World Employment and Social Outlook: trends 2017. International Labour Organization
James O (2009) Evaluating the expectations disconfirmation and expectations anchoring approaches to citizen satisfaction with local public services. J Public Adm Res Theor 19 (1):107–123
Janssen M, Shu W (2008) Transformational government: basics and key issues: a workshop. In: Proceedings of ICEGOV 2008. Cairo, Dec 2008, pp 117–122
Job J (2005) How is trust in government created? It begins at home, but ends in the parliament. Aust Rev Public Aff 6(1):1–23
Kampen JK, Maddens B, Vermunt JK, Salminen A (2003) Trust and satisfaction: a case study of the micro-performance. In: Salminen A (ed) Governing networks: networks: EGPA yearbook. IOS Press, Amsterdam, pp 319–326
Kampen JK, De Walle SV, Bouckaert G (2006) Assessing the relation between satisfaction with public service delivery and trust in government. The impact of the predisposition of citizens toward government on evaluations of its performance. Public Perform Manage Rev 29(4):387–404
Khalil OE (2011) e-Government readiness: does national culture matter? Gov Inf Quart 28(3):388–399
Khan A (2016) Central Bank governance and the role of nonfinancial risk management. In: Working Paper. International Monetary Fund
Kim S, Kim HJ, Lee H (2009) An institutional analysis of an e-government system for anti-corruption: the case of OPEN. Gov Inf Quart 26(1):42–50
Lai Y-L, Cao L, Zhao JS (2010) The impact of political entity on confidence in legal authorities: a comparison between China and Taiwan. J Crim Justice 38(5):934–941
Layne K, Lee J (2001) Developing fully functional e-government. Gov Inf Quart 18(2):122–136
Lee J (2007) Search for stage theory in e-government development. Innovation Public Sect 13:33–48
Maddox W, Lilie S (1984) Beyond liberal and conservative. Cato Institute, Washington
Mahmood M (2016) Enhancing citizens' trust and confidence in government through digital transformation. Int J Electron Gov Res 12(1)
Mahmood, Weerakkody (2014) Digital government diffusion in Bahrain—the role of trust and its influence on adoption. In: Proceedings of the European, Mediterranean & Middle Eastern conference on information systems, 2014

McNeal R, Hale K, Dotterweich L (2008) Citizen–government interaction and the internet: expectations and accomplishments in contact, quality, and trust. J Inf Technol Polit 5(2):213–229
Meijer AJ, Koops BJ, Pieterson W, Overman S, Tije S (2012) Government 2.0: key challenges to its realization. Electron J e-Government 10(1):59–69
Moon MJ, Norris DF (2005) Does managerial orientation matter? The adoption of reinventing government and e-government at the municipal level. Inf Syst J 15(1):43–60
Morgeson FV, Petrescu C (2011) Do they all perform alike? An examination of perceived performance, citizen satisfaction and trust with US federal agencies. Int Rev Admin Sci 77 (3):451–479
Morgeson FV, VanAmburg D, Mithas S (2011) Misplaced trust? Exploring the structure of the e-government-citizen trust relationship. J Public Adm Res Theor 21(2):257–283
Mungiu-Pippidi A, Dadašov R, Fazekas M, Tóth IJ, Kocsis G, Jancsis D, Kortas AM, Kukutschka RMB, Stefavov R, Skolkay A (2016) Public integrity and trust in Europe
Myeong S, Kwon Y, Seo H (2014) Sustainable e-governance: the relationship among trust, digital divide, and e-government. Sustainability 6(9):6049–6069
Nam T (2012) Citizens' attitudes toward open government and government 2.0. Int Rev Admin Sci 78(2):346–368
Navarrete C (2010) Trust in e-government transactional services: a study of citizens' perceptions in Mexico and the US. In: Proceedings of the 43rd Hawaii International Conference on System Sciences (HICSS), 2010. IEEE, pp 1–10
Norquist G (2007) Transparency: the new democracy. Financial Times. Retrieved from www.ft.com/cms/s/2/2206f20c-45c9-11dc-b359-0000779fd2ac.html#axzz1CiOFLwDp
Nye J (1997) In government we don't trust. Foreign Policy 108:99–111
Nye J, Zelikow P, King D (1997) Why people don't trust government. Harvard University Press, Cambridge
Oliver RL (1980) A cognitive model of the antecedents and consequences of satisfaction decisions. J Mark Res 17:460–469
Omar A, Weerakkody V, Sivarajah U (2017) Digitally enabled service transformation in UK public sector: a case analysis of universal credit. Int J Inf Manage 37(4):350–356
O'Neill R (2009) The transformative impact of e-government on public governance in New Zealand. Public Manage Rev 11(6):751–770
Orlikowski WJ (1992) The duality of technology: rethinking the concept of technology in organizations. Organ Sci 3(3):398–427
Orlikowski WJ (2000) Using technology and constituting structures: a practice lens for studying technology in organizations. Organ Sci 11(4):404–428
Orlikowski WJ, Yates J, Okamura K, Fujimoto M (1995) Shaping electronic communication: the metastructuring of technology in the context of use. Organ Sci 6(4):423–444
Orren G (1997) Fall from grace: the public's loss of faith in government. In: Nye J Jr, Zelikow P, King D (eds) Why people don't trust government. Harvard University Press
Osman IH, Anouze A, Irani Z, Lee H, Balcı A, Medeni T, Weerakkody V (2011) A new cobras framework to evaluate e-government services: a citizen centric perspective. In: Tgovernment workshop
Parasuraman A, Zeithaml VA, Berry LL (1988) SERVQUAL: a multiple-item scale for measuring consumer perceptions of service quality. J Retail 64(1):12–40
Parasuraman A, Berry LL, Zeithaml VA (1991) Refinement and reassessment of the SERVQUAL scale. J Retail 67:420–450
Pardo TA, Scholl HJ (2002) Walking atop the cliffs: avoiding failure and avoiding risk in large scale e-government projects. In: Hawai'i international conference on system sciences
Peters BG (1999) American public policy: promise and performance, 5th edn. Chatham House, New York
Pina V, Torres L, Royo S (2009) E-government evolution in EU local governments: a comparative perspective. Online Inf Rev 33(6):1137–1168
Poister TH, Henry GT (1994) Citizen ratings of public and private service quality: a comparative perspective. Public Adm Rev 54(2):155–160

Rodrigues G, Sarabdeen J, Balasubramanian S (2016) Factors that influence consumer adoption of e-government services in the UAE: a UTAUT model perspective. J Internet Commer 15(1):18–39
Salmi M, Hasnan N (2016) E-Government technology acceptance analysis of citizens: sultanate of Oman case. Int J Soc Relevance Concern 4(1):13–26
Sargeant A, Lee S (2002) Improving public trust in the voluntary sector: an empirical analysis. Int J Nonprofit Voluntary Sect Mark 7(1):68–83
Scharpf F (1999) Governing in Europe: effective and democratic. Oxford University Press, Oxford
Scholl HJ (2001) Applying stakeholder theory to e-government. In: Schmidt B, Stanoevska-Slabeva K, Tschammer V (eds) Towards the e-society: e-commerce, e-business and e-government. Kluwer Academic Publishers, Norwell
Scott M, Golden W, Hughes M (2004) The implementation of citizen-centred e-government: a stakeholder viewpoint. In: Working paper. Centre for Innovation & Structural Change, National University of Ireland, Galway
Seifert JW, Chung J (2009) Using e-government to reinforce government—citizen relationships: comparing government reform in the United States and China. Soc Sci Comput Rev 27(1):3–23
Shafi AS, Weerakkody V (2009) Understanding citizens' behavioural intention in the adoption of e-government services in the state of Qatar. In: ECIS, pp 1618–1629
Sharma SK, Govindaluri SM, Gattoufi S (2015) Understanding and predicting the quality determinants of e-government services: a two-staged regression-neural network model. J Model Manage 10(3):325–340
Siau K, Long Y (2005) Synthesizing e-government stage models—a meta-synthesis based on meta-ethnography approach. Ind Manage Data Syst 105(4):443–458
Siddique W (2016) Critical success factors affecting e-government policy implementation in Pakistan. JeDEM-eJournal of eDemocracy and Open Government 8(1):102–126
Song C, Lee J (2013) Can social media restore citizen trust in government? In: Public management research conference. Madison, pp 20–22
Srivastava SC, Teo TS (2009) Citizen trust development for e-government adoption and usage: insights from young adults in Singapore. In: Communications of the association for information systems, vol 25
Tennert JR, Schroeder AD (1999) Stakeholder Analysis. In: Paper presented at the 60th annual meeting of the American society for public administration, Orlando
Teo TS, Srivastava SC, Jiang L (2008) Trust and electronic government success: an empirical study. J Manage Inf Syst 25(3):99–132
Tolbert CJ, Mossberger K (2006) The effects of e-government on trust and confidence in government. Public Adm Rev 66(3):354–369
United Nations (2012) E-government survey 2012: e-government for the people. Department of Economic and Social Affairs Division for Public Administration and Development Management
United Nations (2014) E-government survey 2014: e-government for the future we want. Department of Economic and Social Affairs Division for Public Administration and Development Management
United Nations (2016) E-government survey 2016: e-government in support of sustainable development. Department of Economic and Social Affairs Division for Public Administration and Development Management
Uslaner EM (2001) Is Washington really the problem? In: Hibbing JR, Thesis-Morse E (eds) What is it about government that americans dislike? Cambridge University Press, New York
Van de Walle S, Bouckaert G (2003) Public service performance and trust in government: the problem of causality. Int J Public Adm 26(8–9):891–913
Van de Walle S, Van Roosbroek S, Bouckaert G (2008) Trust in the public sector: is there any evidence for a long-term decline? Int Rev Admin Sci 74(1):47–64
Van Ryzin GG, Muzzio D, Immerwahr S, Gulick L, Martinez E (2004) Drivers and consequences of citizen satisfaction: an application of the American customer satisfaction index model to New York City. Public Adm Rev 64(3):331–341

Waller P, Weerakkody V (2016) Digital government: overcoming the systemic failure of transformation. In Working paper 2. Brunel University, London

Weerakkody V, Janssen M, Dwivedi Y (eds) (2009) Handbook of research on ICT enabled transformational government: a global perspective. Information Science Reference, Hershey

Weerakkody V, El-Haddadeh R, Al-Sobhi F, Shareef MA, Dwivedi YK (2013) Examining the influence of intermediaries in facilitating e-government adoption: an empirical investigation. Int J Inf Manage 33(5):716–725

Weerakkody V, Omar A, El-Haddadeh R (2016) Digitally-enabled service transformation in the public sector: the lure of institutional pressure and strategic response towards change. Gov Inf Quart 33(4):658–668

Welch EW, Hinnant CC, Moon MJ (2005) Linking citizen satisfaction with e-government and trust in government. J Public Adm Res Theor 15(3):371–391

West DM (2004) E-government and the transformation of service delivery and citizen attitudes. Public Adm Rev 64(1):15–27

Wolak J, Palus CK (2010) The dynamics of public confidence in US state and local government. State Polit Policy Quart 10(4):421–445

World Bank (2010) Results, performance budgeting and trust in government. Washington

Yamin M, Mattar R (2016) e-Government in Saudi Arabia—an empirical study. BVICAM's Int J Inf Technol 8(1):944–949

Zouridis S, Thaens M (2003) E-government: towards a public administration approach. Asian J Public Adm 25(2):159–183

Zwahr T, Finger M, Müller P (2005) More than digitisation-The transformative potential of e-governance: an exploratory case study. In: Proceedings of the 38th Annual Hawaii International Conference on System Sciences, 2005, HICSS'05. IEEE, p 127

Chapter 3
Conceptual Model

3.1 Introduction

Chapter 2 provided an insight on the challenges faced by the government in dealing with the decline of citizens' trust and confidence in government over the last decades. Review of the literature showed that there is a lack of knowledge on how digital transformation of government can reverse the decline in citizens' trust and confidence. Additionally, factors that were already investigated by other researchers have been identified as factors influencing citizens' trust and confidence and transformation of government. This chapter presents the proposed hypotheses to investigate how digital transformation of government influences citizens' trust and confidence in government.

This chapter is structured as follows. Sections 3.2–3.9 describe the relationships between different variables of the proposed conceptual model, which is presented in Sect. 3.10. Finally, Sect. 3.11, summarizes the overall chapter.

3.2 Relationship Between E-Government and Transformation of Government

E-government has been widely investigated by various researchers, and trust has been identified as a key factor in the adoption of e-government services (Al-Khouri 2012; Al-Shafi and Weerakkody 2010; Osman et al. 2011). Literature shows that e-government has been investigated in relation to citizens' trust through different models. For example, Morgeson and Petrescu (2011) consider e-government as a performance antecedent, mediated by satisfaction towards citizen trust and confidence. Bannister and Connolly (2011) have also investigated the direct relationship of e-government with citizens' trust and confidence in government. West (2004), on the other hand, recommended the relationship between e-government and

M. Mahmood, *Does Digital Transformation of Government Lead to Enhanced Citizens' Trust and Confidence in Government?*, Springer Theses,
https://doi.org/10.1007/978-3-030-01759-0_3

transformation of government. The existing studies did not investigate the relationship with transformation of government, leading to the citizens' trust and confidence in government (see Table 3.1).

From the above discussion, the following hypothesis is drawn:

H1a E-government positively influences transformation of government

3.3 Relationship Between Technology and Transformation of Government

Some researchers pointed out that there is need to investigate the relationship between technology and citizens' trust and confidence in government. Other researchers (Bannister and Connolly 2011; Waller and Weerakkody 2016) highlighted the important role of technology in changing government policies by being a part of the policy design process, which is also considered as transformation of government. In line with this argument, there is a need to investigate the relationship of technology with transformation of government, which is predicted to have an influence on citizens' trust and confidence in government. The models developed by Morgenson et al. (2011) and Morgeson and Petrescu (2011) did not focus on technology as recommended by various other authors (Bannister and Connolly 2011; Hiller and Belanger 2001; Waller and Weerakkody 2016).

H1b Technology positively influences transformation of government

3.4 Relationship Between Citizen Expectations and Transformation of Government

Citizens' expectation was defined by Parasuraman et al. (1988) as what the customers think or have an idea of the services should offer. This argument was supported by Nam (2012) by highlighting that public expectation which is considered in this study, as citizens' expectation is the most determining factor that facilitates decline in the public's trust of government. For instance, (Morgeson et al. 2011) investigated the relationship between citizens' expectation, satisfaction, citizens' trust and confidence in the agency and Wessington. Morgeson et al. (2011) study focused on the relationship between citizens' expectation and citizens' satisfaction leading to citizens' trust and confidence in government.

It is clear from the arguments presented above and Chap. 2 that citizen expectations have a direct or indirect relationship with transformation of government. However, as stated previously, hardly any studies have considered the relationship between transformation of government (Bannister and Connolly 2011) and citizens'

Table 3.1 Theoretical background for the drawn relationships

Construct	Hypothesis #	Relationship affected	Supporting authors for the relationship	Supporting theories
EGOV	H1a	EGOV → TRANSF	Andersen and Henriksen (2006); Bannister and Connolly (2011); Baum and Di Maio (2000); Bellamy and Taylor (1998); Bonham et al. (2001); Coursey and Norris (2008); Layne and Lee (2001)	Public administration theory (Zouridis and Thaens 2003); Institutional theory (Bekkers and Meijer 2012; Kim et al. 2009; Luna-Reyes and Gil-García 2011; Pina et al. 2009; Weerakkody et al. 2016) Structuration Theory (Orlikowski 1992, 2000; Orlikowski et al. 1995; Meijer et al. 2012) User adoption theories (example Technology Acceptance Model, TAM and Diffusion of Innovation, DOI) (see Gilbert and Balestrini 2004)
TECH	H1b	TECH → TRANSF	Bannister and Connolly (2011); Bingham (2010); Bonham et al. (2001); Kim et al. (2009); Weerakkody et al. (2009)	Public administration theory (Zouridis and Thaens 2003); Institutional theory (Bekkers and Meijer 2012; Kim et al. 2009; Luna-Reyes and Gil-García 2011; Pina et al. 2009; Weerakkody et al. 2016) Structuration Theory (Orlikowski 1992, 2000; Orlikowski et al. 1995; Meijer et al. 2012) User adoption theories (example Technology Acceptance Model, TAM and Diffusion of Innovation, DOI) (see Gilbert and Balestrini 2004)

(continued)

Table 3.1 (continued)

Construct	Hypothesis #	Relationship affected	Supporting authors for the relationship	Supporting theories
TRANSPY	H1c	TRANSPY → TRANSF	Brown (1999); Fountain (2001); Northrup and Thorson (2003)	Public administration theory (Zouridis and Thaens 2003); Agent-principal theory (Kim et al. 2009) Institutional theory (Kim et al. 2009; Weerakkody et al. 2016)
ACOUNT	H1d	ACOUNT → TRANSF	Bannister and Connolly (2011); Bingham (2010); Demchak et al. (2000); Kauvar (1998); Norquist (2007)	Public administration theory (Zouridis and Thaens 2003); Agent-principal theory (Kim et al. 2009) Institutional theory (Kim et al. 2009; Weerakkody et al. 2016)
EXPEC	H1e	EXPEC → TRANSF	Dalton (2005); Graham and Avery (2013); Seifert and Petersen (2002); Welch et al. (2005)	Stakeholder theory (Chan et al. 2003; Pardo and Scholl 2002; Scholl 2001; Tennert and Schroeder 1999)
TRANSF	H2	TRANSF → PERFO	Chatfield (2009); Fang (2002); Florini (2000); Kim et al. (2009)	Public Administration Theory (Zouridis and Thaens 2003)
PERFO	H3	PERFO → SATISF	Bouckaert et al. (2005); Heintzman and Marson (2005); Kampen et al. (2006); Osman et al. (2011); Tolbert and Mossberger (2006); Van de Walle and Bouckaert (2003); Van de Walle et al. (2008)	Micro-Performance Theory (Kampen et al. 2003, 2006; Van de Walle and Bouckaert 2003)
SATISF	H4	SATISF → TRUST & CONFIDENCE	Bannister and Connolly (2011); Bouckaert et al. (2005); Heintzman and Marson (2005); Kampen et al. (2006); Tolbert and Mossberger (2006); Osman et al. (2011); Van de Walle and Bouckaert (2003); Van de Walle et al. (2008); Welch et al. (2005)	Micro-Performance Theory (Kampen et al. 2003, 2006; Van de Walle and Bouckaert 2003)
TRUST & CONFIDENCE	—	—	—	Micro-Performance Theory (Van de Walle and Bouckaert 2003) Exit-Voice Theory (Fornell et al. 1996; Hirschman 1970; Morgeson et al. 2011)

trust and confidence in government which provides a solid justification of investigating this relationship through the below hypothesis (see Table 3.1).

From the above discussion, the following hypothesis can be drawn:

H1c Expectation positively influences transformation of government

3.5 Relationship Between Transparency and Transformation of Government

Transparency is a measure or a tool for an outsider to assess the true operations undertaken by a company (Chen et al. 2003). Many studies (Bannister and Connolly 2011; O'Neill 2009; Tolbert and Mossberger 2006; Waller and Weerakkody 2016) highlighted the necessity of transparency in building citizen trust and confidence. In a similar argument, other studies (Chen et al. 2003; Mahmood and Weerakkody 2014; Song and Lee 2013; Welch et al. 2005) argued that transparency works closely with e-government towards transformation of government. Thus, the following hypothesis is drawn:

H1d Transparency positively influences transformation of government

3.6 Relationship Between Accountability and Transformation of Government

Some researchers stated that accountability works closely with transparency, and cannot be neglected (Amaliah et al. 2015; Bannister and Connolly 2011; Kim et al. 2009). Accountability was defined differently by researchers; for instance, Chen et al. (2003) looked at accountability from a decision-making and characteristic aspect, rather than operational. Various researchers argued that transparency and accountability are related (Amaliah et al. 2015; Bannister and Connolly 2011; Kim et al. 2009), and yet, hardly any research included both accountability and transparency to test citizens' trust and confidence in government. It was further argued that both accountability and transparency could influence the transformation of government (Bannister and Connolly 2011).

From the above discussion, the following hypothesis is drawn:

H1e Accountability positively influences transformation of government

3.7 Relationship Between Transformation of Government and Performance

Bannister and Connolly (2011) stated that government transformation is described as a fluid and yet a question in the literature is left unanswered that is the relationship between transformation of government and citizens' trust and confidence in government. Janssen and Shu (2008) defined transformational government as transparent, accountable, efficient, and agile. There is no clear understanding of the elements of transformation of government, and how it influences citizen trust and confidence in government. In line with arguments from Bannister and Connolly (2011) and Janssen and Shu (2008), it was predicted that transformation of government influences performance of government, which leads to citizen trust and confidence.

As stated earlier, the relationship between e-government and transformation of government needs to be investigated (West 2004) which is drawn as **H1a**; the relationship between technology and transformation of government, also defined by Hiller and Belanger (2001) and Waller and Weerakkody (2016) is drawn as **H1b**; the relationship between citizen expectation and transformation of government (Bannister and Connolly 2011; Morgeson et al. 2011) is drawn as **H1c**; the relationship between transparency and transformation of government (Chen et al. 2003; Mahmood and Weerakkody 2014; Song and Lee 2013; Welch et al. 2005) is drawn as **H1d**; and the relationship between accountability and transformation of government (Amaliah et al. 2015; Bannister and Connolly 2011; Kim et al. 2009) is drawn as **H1e**. All these hypotheses will be investigated on how they work with transformation of government, leading to citizens' trust and confidence, mediated by performance of government and citizens' satisfaction.

From the above discussion, the following hypothesis is drawn:

H2 Transformation of government positively influences performance of government

3.8 Relationship Between Performance of Government and Satisfaction

According to Hudson (2006), performance plays a role towards trust in the government, which is supported by other researchers (Abramson 1983; Maddox and Lilie 1984; Nye et al. 1997). The models developed by Morgeson et al. (2011) and Morgeson and Petrescu (2011) also support this argument, as various antecedents were tested as a part of performance, mediated by satisfaction leading to citizens' trust and confidence in government. However, Morgeson and Petrescu (2011) defined service, technology, e-government, expectations, age, education, income and gender as performance antecedents. This research proposes to test the relationship between performance of government and satisfaction leading to citizens' trust and confidence, taking into account the relationship between transformation of government and other working factors defined above.

From the above discussion, the following hypothesis is drawn:

H3 Performance of Government positively influences citizens' satisfaction in government

3.9 Relationship Between Satisfaction and Citizens' Trust and Confidence in Government

While researchers are still investigating the possible relationship between e-government and citizens' declining trust in government, models that can provide a solution to this are still in their early stages. For instance, Morgeson et al. (2011) investigated the relationship between the Internet and trust in Washington (US), mediated by e-government and influenced by other factors. However, the authors could not establish a significant relationship with trust in government. On the other hand, Morgeson and Petrescu (2011) developed an extended model, with related components of performance as antecedents toward citizens' satisfaction. Other studies (Bannister and Connolly 2011; West 2004) highlighted the importance of transformation of government, which is predicted to lead to citizens' trust and confidence in government.

Similar results were arrived at by another piece of research conducted by Teo et al. (2008). It investigated the relationship between trust in government and e-government on one hand, and user satisfaction and intention to use e-government, on the other, using trust as the independent variable rather than dependent. It can thus be concluded that satisfaction and trust affect citizen engagement with government. Satisfaction is influenced by performance, and performance is affected by a number of aspects, including technology that is used in the government, the use of e-government as a tool, and citizens' expectations of the government. When these three aspects are involved, a traditional government setup will not be the same and change has to be brought in, with transparency becoming another important factor that is needed in the government.

Therefore, e-government, technology and expectation need to be linked to transformation. However, transformation without transparency and accountability is unlikely to improve performance (Bannister and Connolly 2011). Therefore, transformation must be influenced by transparency and accountability (Bannister and Connolly 2011; Kim et al. 2009). Transformation here is considered an independent variable that is expected to increase citizens' engagement with their governments, which is the dependent variable. However, the relationship between independent and dependent variables is affected by mediating variables (Morgeson et al. 2011). Two such variables that have been identified by previous researchers are government performance and satisfaction of citizens (Kim et al. 2009;

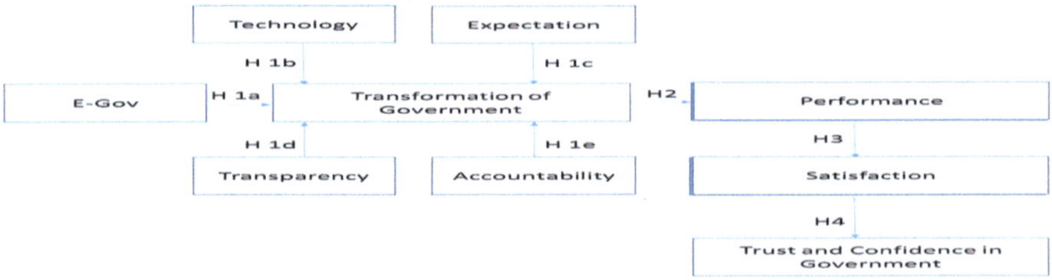

Fig. 3.1 Proposed conceptual model

Morgeson et al. 2011; Norquist 2007; Tolbert and Mossberger 2006; Welch et al. 2005; West 2004). From the above argument, it is clear that trust and confidence in government will be the dependent variable in this model; this relationship is supported by Bannister and Connolly (2011) and Morgeson et al. (2011).

From the above discussion, the following hypothesis is drawn:

H4 Satisfaction positively influences citizens' trust and confidence in government

3.10 The Proposed Conceptual Model and Extracted Theories

From the above arguments and drawn hypotheses, the following conceptual model is proposed in this research (Fig. 3.1), with the theoretical background presented in Table 3.1.

It is worth highlighting that this research adopts a citizen centric perspective, which means that this research is about citizens' perceptions of all constructs and hypotheses proposed in the conceptual model.

3.11 Summary

This chapter provided the background for the conceptual model and proposed hypotheses supported by arguments highlighted in literature review. Majority of the studies and models focused on technical, service quality, usability and adoption aspects of ICT-enabled transformation projects with limited impact on practice and no real transformation of government. For instance, there were no fundamental changes to the way core government functions were performed to achieve noticeable gains in performance and efficiency. As a result, citizens' trust and confidence has continued to decline. Therefore, there is a need for better understating how transformation of government as a construct affects citizens' trust and confidence in government, in the presence of other factors such as e-government, technology, citizen expectations, transparency, accountability, government performance and citizen satisfaction. This research bridges the aforementioned gap by proposing a conceptual model, which is a first of its kind to investigate the relationship between transformation of government and citizens' trust and confidence in government. The next chapter will present the methodology that will be followed to investigate this conceptual model.

References

Abramson Paul (1983) Political attitudes in America. Freeman, San Francisco, CA

Al-Khouri AM (2012) eGovernment strategies the case of the United Arab Emirates (UAE). Eur J ePractice 17:126–150

Al-Shafi S, Weerakkody V (2010) Factors affecting e-government adoption in the state of Qatar. In: Proceedings of the European and mediterranean conference on information systems, Abu Dhabi, UAE, 12–13 April 2010

Amaliah Said I, Iaafar NH, Atan R (2015) Assessing accountability in government linked companies: an empirical evidence. Int Bus Manage 9(4):460–469

Andersen KV, Henriksen HZ (2006) E-government maturity models: extension of the Layne and Lee model. Gov Inf Q 23(2):236–248

Bannister F, Connolly R (2011) Trust and transformational government: a proposed framework for research. Gov Inf Q 28(2):137–147

Baum C, Di Maio A (2000) Gartner's four phases of e-government. Gartner Group, New York

Bekkers V, Meijer A (2012) A meta-theory of e-government. In: 34th EGPA conference proceedings

Bellamy C, Taylor J (1998) Governing in the information age. Open University Press, Buckingham, UK; Bristol, PA

Bingham LB (2010) Online deliberation and the United States open government initiative. Online Deliberation, 53

Bonham G, Seifert J, Thorson S (2001) The transformational potential of e-government: the role of political leadership. In: 4th Pan European international relations conference, 8–11 September, 2001. University of Kent, UK

Bouckaert G, Van de Walle S, Kampen JK (2005) Potential for comparative public opinion research in public administration. Int Rev Admin Sci 71(2):229–240

Brown D (1999) Information systems for improved performance management: development approaches in US public agency. In: Heeks R (ed) Reinventing government in the information age. Routledge, New York, pp 321–330

Chan CML, Shan-Ling P, Tan C-W (2003) Managing stakeholder relationships in an e-government project. In: Ninth Americas conference on information systems, Florida

Chatfield AT (2009) Public service reform through e-government: a case study of 'e-Tax' in Japan. Electron J E-Gov 7(2):135–146

Chen KC, Wei KC, Chen Z (2003) Disclosure, corporate governance, and the cost of equity capital: evidence from Asia's emerging markets. Corporate governance, and the cost of equity capital: evidence from Asia's emerging markets. Retrieved from http://dx.doi.org/10.2139/ssrn.422000

Coursey D, Norris DF (2008) Models of e-government: are they correct? An empirical assessment. Public Adm Rev 68(3):523–536

Dalton RJ (2005) The social transformation of trust in government. Int Rev Sociol 15(1):133–154

Demchak CC, Friis C, La Porte TM (2000) Webbing governance: national differences in constructing the public face. In: Garson GD (ed) Handbook of public information systems. Marcel Dekker, New York

Fang Z (2002) E-government in digital era: concept, practice, and development. Int J Comput Internet and Manag 10(2):1–22

Florini A (2000) Does the invisible hand need a transparent glove? The politics of transparency. World Bank Annual Conf Dev Econ 163–184

Fornell C, Johnson MD, Anderson EW, Cha J, Bryant BE (1996) The American customer satisfaction index: nature, purpose and findings. J Mark 60(4):7–18

Fountain J (2001) Building the virtual state: information technology and institutional change. Brookings Institution Press, Washington, DC7

Gilbert D, Balestrini P (2004) Barriers and benefits in the adoption of e-government. Int J Public Sect Manage 17(4):286–301

Graham M, Avery EJ (2013) Government public relations and social media: an analysis of the perceptions and trends of social media use at the local government level. Public Relat J 7(4):1–21

Heintzman R, Marson B (2005) People, service and trust: is there a public sector service value chain? Int Rev Admin Sci 71(4):549–575

Hiller JS, Belanger F (2001) Privacy strategies for electronic government. E-government series. The PricewaterhouseCoopers Endowment for the Business of Government. Available at http://www.businessofgovernment.org/pdfs/HillerReport.pdf

Hirschman AO (1970) Exit, voice, and loyalty: responses to decline in firms, organizations, and states, vol 25. Harvard university press

Hudson J (2006) Institutional trust and subjective well-being across the EU. Kyklos 59(1):43–62

Janssen M, Shu W (2008) Transformational government: basics and key issues: a workshop. In: Proceedings of ICEGOV 2008, December 1–4, Cairo, Egypt, pp 117–122

Kampen JK, Maddens B, Vermunt JK, Salminen A (2003) Trust and satisfaction: a case study of the micro-performance. In: Salminen A (ed) Governing networks: networks: EGPA Yearbook. IOS Press, Amsterdam, pp 319–326

Kampen JK, De Walle SV, Bouckaert G (2006) Assessing the relation between satisfaction with public service delivery and trust in government. the impact of the predisposition of citizens toward government on evaluations of its performance. Public Perform Manage Rev 29(4): 387–404

Kauvar G (1998) Electronic government: concepts, visions, and strategies. In: The KAPAs international symposium on electronic government: visions and strategies, Seoul, Korea

Kim S, Kim HJ, Lee H (2009) An institutional analysis of an e-government system for anti-corruption: the case of OPEN. Gov Inf Q 26(1):42–50

Layne K, Lee J (2001) Developing fully functional e-government. Gov Inf Q 18(2):122–136

Maddox William, Lilie Stuart (1984) Beyond liberal and conservative. Cato Institute, Washington, DC

Mahmood, Weerakkody (2014) Digital government diffusion in Bahrain – the role of trust and its influence on adoption. In: Proceedings of the European, mediterranean & middle eastern conference on information systems, 2014

Meijer AJ, Koops BJ, Pieterson W, Overman S, Tije S (2012) Government 2.0: key challenges to its realization. Electron J E-Gov 10(1):59–69

Morgeson FV, Petrescu C (2011) Do they all perform alike? An examination of perceived performance, citizen satisfaction and trust with US federal agencies. Int Rev Admin Sci 77(3): 451–479

Morgeson FV, VanAmburg D, Mithas S (2011) Misplaced trust? Exploring the structure of the e-government-citizen trust relationship. J Public Adm Res Theor 21(2):257–283

Nam T (2012) Citizens' attitudes toward open government and government 2.0. Int Rev Admin Sci 78(2):346–368

Norquist G (2007) Transparency: the new democracy. Financial Times. Retrieved from www.ft.com/cms/s/2/2206f20c-45c911dc-b359-0000779fd2ac.html#axzz1CiOFLwDp

Northrup TA, Thorson SJ (2003) The web of governance and democratic accountability. In: Proceedings of the 36th annual Hawaii international conference on system sciences
Nye Joseph, Zelikow Philip, King David (1997) Why people don't trust government. Harvard University Press, Cambridge, MA
O'Neill R (2009) The transformative impact of e-government on public governance in New Zealand. Public Manag Rev 11(6):751–770
Orlikowski WJ (1992) The duality of technology: rethinking the concept of technology in organizations. Organ Sci 3(3):398–427
Orlikowski WJ (2000) Using technology and constituting structures: a practice lens for studying technology in organizations. Organ Sci 11(4):404–428
Orlikowski WJ, Yates J, Okamura K, Fujimoto M (1995) Shaping electronic communication: the metastructuring of technology in the context of use. Organ Sci 6(4):423–444
Osman IH, Anouze A, Irani Z, Lee H, Balcı A, Medeni T, Weerakkody V (2011) A new cobras framework to evaluate e-government services: a citizen centric perspective. In Tgovernment workshop
Parasuraman A, Zeithaml Valerie A, Berry Leonard L (1988) SERVQUAL: a multiple-item scale for measuring consumer perceptions of service quality. J Retail 64(1):12–40
Pardo TA, Scholl HJ (2002) Walking atop the cliffs: avoiding failure and avoiding risk in large scale e-government projects. In: Hawai'i international conference on system sciences
Pina V, Torres L, Royo S (2009) E-government evolution in EU local governments: a comparative perspective. Online Inf Rev 33(6):1137–1168
Scholl HJ (2001) Applying stakeholder theory to e-government. In: Schmidt B, Stanoevska-Slabeva K, Tschammer V (eds) Towards the e-society: e-commerce, e-business and e-government. Kluwer Academic Publishers, Norwell, MA
Seifert JW, Petersen RE (2002) The promise of all things E? Expectations and challenges of emergent electronic government. Perspect Glob Dev Technol 1(2):193–212
Song C, Lee J (2013) Can social media restore citizen trust in government? Public management research conference. Madison, WI, pp 20–22
Tennert JR, Schroeder AD (1999) Stakeholder analysis. In: Paper presented at the 60th annual meeting of the American Society for Public Administration, Orlando, Florida
Teo TS, Srivastava SC, Jiang L (2008) Trust and electronic government success: an empirical study. J Manage Inf Syst 25(3):99–132
Tolbert CJ, Mossberger K (2006) The effects of e-government on trust and confidence in government. Public Adm Rev 66(3):354–369
Van de Walle S, Bouckaert G (2003) Public service performance and trust in government: the problem of causality. Int J Public Adm 26(8–9):891–913
Van de Walle S, Van Roosbroek S, Bouckaert G (2008) Trust in the public sector: is there any evidence for a long-term decline? Int Rev Admin Sci 74(1):47–64
Waller P, Weerakkody V (2016) Digital government: overcoming the systemic failure of transformation. Working Paper 2. Brunel University, London
Weerakkody V, Janssen M, Dwivedi Y (eds) (2009) Handbook of research on ICT enabled transformational government: a global perspective. Inf Sci Ref, Hershey, PA
Weerakkody V, Omar A, El-Haddadeh R (2016) Digitally-enabled service transformation in the public sector: the lure of institutional pressure and strategic response towards change. Gov Inf Q 33(4):658–668
Welch EW, Hinnant CC, Moon MJ (2005) Linking citizen satisfaction with e-government and trust in government. J Public Adm Res Theor 15(3):371–391
West DM (2004) E-government and the transformation of service delivery and citizen attitudes. Public Adm Rev 64(1):15–27
Zouridis S, Thaens M (2003) E-government: towards a public administration approach. Asian J Public Adm 25(2):159–183

Chapter 4
Research Methodology

4.1 Introduction

Chapter 3 presents the conceptual model along with eight hypotheses for investigating the influence of transformation of government on citizens' trust and confidence from citizens' perspective. In this chapter, the research methodology is presented that includes amongst other elements research philosophy and design. Elements of this chapter are very important for this research, and thus the selection of suitable methodology will be based on a thorough review of available options.

This research is explanatory by nature and positivism will form the governing philosophical paradigm for this study. A quantitative approach will be employed for this research. The target audiences are the ordinary citizens living in the Kingdom of Bahrain, who were approached randomly through the development and distribution of an online survey through different means such as email, SMS and social media applications. Prior to launching the main survey, pre-test and pilot test were performed to validate the conceptual model and hypotheses, and to ensure the reliability of the collected data.

This chapter is structured as follows. Section 4.2 is about the three research philosophies and justifies the selection of positivism. Section 4.3 discusses different elements of research design: research purpose, unit of analysis, research data, mode of observation and the time dimension. The six stages of the research process are also illustrated in this section. Comparisons between quantitative and qualitative methodologies, as well as the selection of quantitative approach for this research are provided in Sect. 4.4. As for Sect. 4.5, it discusses sampling process, data collection tool and different types of questionnaires. Questionnaire development and validation phase is covered in Sect. 4.6 along with the results of validity and reliability tests applied following the pilot test. The justifications for selection of SEM are highlighted in Sect. 4.7. Section 4.8 deals with issues related to ethics approval, with conclusions outlined in Sect. 4.9.

M. Mahmood, *Does Digital Transformation of Government Lead to Enhanced Citizens' Trust and Confidence in Government?*, Springer Theses,
https://doi.org/10.1007/978-3-030-01759-0_4

4.2 Research Philosophy

Prior to selecting the research method and commencing with the research design, it is important to select the appropriate research philosophy, as it establishes the foundation for what follows (Creswell 2009). There are three key research philosophical/epistemology approaches/assumptions: positivist, interpretive, and critical research (Mingers 2001, 2003; Orlikowski and Baroudi 1991). The two main approaches used in the IS research are positivist and interpretive (Chen and Hirschheim 2004; Gregor 2006; Guba and Lincoln 1994; Orlikowski and Baroudi 1991; Myers and Avison 1997). However, amongst the two approaches, positivist is considered as the most popular one in IS research (Mingers 2003; Orlikowski and Baroudi 1991; Straub et al. 2004; Yin 2003, 2009). As for critical research, it is rarely used in IS literature, as it is applicable to researches where the focus is on conflicts and contradictions.

Positivism is used to test theory for understanding a certain phenomenon that is in question (Orlikowski and Baroudi 1991). It is mainly associated with facts, figures, measures and numbers as opposed to researchers' beliefs and values (Bryman and Bell 2007; Howe 1988; Weber 2004). The quantitative research method is used where for example, theory is tested, conceptual model is developed, hypotheses are suggested and validated, data is collected and analysed (Bryman and Bell 2007; Saunders et al. 2011). On the other hand, interpretive approach attempts to understand a certain phenomenon through accessing the 'meaning' participants have about the phenomenon (Orlikowski and Baroudi 1991; Walsham 1995). It is mainly associated with beliefs and intentions researches' have as opposed to positivism, which is based on figures and measures (Howe 1988; Orlikowski and Baroudi 1991; Weber 2004). The qualitative research method is used where for example case studies, interviews and ethnographic methods are adopted (Weber 2004).

Both positivism and interpretive approaches are explaining or reflecting reality, whereas the critical research approach is about developing/creating/changing reality and promoting emancipation (Niehaves and Bernd 2006; Orlikowski and Baroudi 1991). Additionally, it questions or criticizes the reality and the knowledge gained in an effective and efficient way. As for the used methodology for critical research, there is no single agreed methodology; however, it is close to some extant to the interpretive approach (Niehaves and Bernd 2006). For instance, in the IS research, the discussed topics in the previous studies were power, gender, digital divide and IS failure (Niehaves and Bernd 2006). In this regard, critical research is rarely adopted and can be considered as a missing approach or paradigm (Chen and Hirschheim 2004; Richardson and Robinson 2007).

In light of the above discussion related to the three philosophy approaches, the most appropriate one for the research is positivism. The reasons for this selection are: this research is explaining a reality and not attempting to create a new reality and as such, the third approach that is the critical research philosophy is eliminated from the selection. Secondly, it is about understanding and investigating a phenomenon by testing a current theory and not about understanding a certain phenomenon through accessing the 'meaning' participants have about the phenomenon. As such, the second research philosophy that is the interpretive is eliminated. Third, this research adopts quantitative research methodology, develops, and validates a conceptual model that is building up on previous theoretical frameworks and models. The research is related to investigating the influence of transformation of government on citizens' trust and confidence in government. As such, the research aim, objectives, research questions, conceptual model and hypotheses indicate that positivism is a more suitable philosophy for this research.

4.3 Research Design

Prior to selecting research methodology, and collecting and analyzing the data, it is very critical to agree on the appropriate research design to be followed throughout the different phases of this research. Research design here refers to a framework or systematic approach to be adopted to fulfil the aim and objectives of this research (Avison et al. 1999; Bryman 2004; Bryman and Bell 2007; Creswell 2003; Gable 1994; Jick 1979). The key elements of research design are explained in the subsections below.

4.3.1 Research Purpose

The three types of research purpose are exploratory, descriptive, and explanatory (Robson 2002; Sekaran 2003). Exploratory research is about exploring the phenomena through understanding the problem and looking for ideas and insights (Robson 2002). It comes with qualitative research methodology, where interviews and focus groups are often used. The second type is the descriptive research and from its name, it is clear that researchers look for an accurate description of the phenomena in question (Robson 2002). As opposed to exploratory research, the key variables are defined, and either a quantitative or qualitative approach can be used (Robson 2002). The third type is the explanatory research, which is also known as hypothesis testing or casual relationship. From its names, it is clear that the key variables and relationships are defined, and a quantitative research methodology is associated with it. Accordingly, it is about explaining the phenomena in question through testing the defined hypothesis between variables so that the relationships between these variables can be explained (Robson 2002; Saunders 2011).

In addition to investigating the relationship between transformation of government and citizens' trust and confidence in government, this research identifies factors that influence transformation of government and determines the relationships amongst these factors. In doing so, a conceptual model along with hypotheses is developed, validated and tested here. As per the above definitions, the purpose of this research is explanatory, as it explains and predicts relationships amongst defined variables and hypotheses of the developed conceptual model.

4.3.2 Unit of Analysis

This research investigates the influence of transformation of government on citizens' trust, and citizens' confidence in the government. As such, the target audience is the citizen, who is the unit of analysis for this research.

4.3.3 Research Data

There are two types of research data, which are primary and secondary (Collis and Hussey 2003). Primary research data is the data collected by the researcher for addressing the research aim, objectives and questions to be answered (Collis and Hussey 2003). Surveys, case studies, laboratory experiment and action research, for instance, can be used to collect such data (Bryman and Bell 2007; Orlikowski and Baroudi 1991). The second type is the secondary data, where the collected data is not related directly to the research in hand such as published summaries, reports and statistics. The secondary data may be suitable when there is a need to conduct a comparative research nationally or internationally. The choice between the primary data and secondary data is based on the research questions to be addressed. For instance, some researches may need to use primary data, while others only need secondary data. In some cases, both primary and secondary data maybe used (Saunders 2011).

In order to address the research questions set for this research, primary data is used for collecting the related data. In particular, data related to every defined construct within the conceptual model for this study will be collected from people living in the Kingdom of Bahrain.

4.3.4 Choice of Research Design (Mode of Observation)

There are four key types of research design: survey, case study, laboratory experiment and action research (Orlikowski and Baroudi 1991). Since the unit of analysis for this research is the citizen, survey mode will be the suitable choice. This will enable data to be collected from a large number of citizens, which will become very difficult with the other three options. Quantitative research methodology rather than the qualitative method fits better with the survey mode of observation. More details on the survey approach can be found in Sect. 4.5 of this chapter.

4.3.5 Time Dimension

With survey chosen to be the selected mode of observation for this research, the next question is whether the survey should be conducted once at a defined time, or more than once over a given period of time (Bryman and Bell 2007; Churchill and

Dawn 1999; Sekaran 2003). The aim, objectives, questions, limited budget and timeframe defined for the accomplishment of this research make the choice of a cross-sectional survey better suited than a longitudinal survey. This choice is consistent with similar studies conducted previously in IS research (e.g. Morgeson et al. 2011; Teo et al. 2008; Tolbert and Mossberger 2006).

4.3.6 *Stages of the Research Process*

This section provides an overview of the process followed for accomplishing this research, with the details of each stage and process covered in different chapters of this thesis. Figure 4.1 illustrates that this research was conducted in six stages: (a) literature review, (b) development of conceptual model, (c) research design, (d) data collection, (e) data analysis and (f) discussion of findings and key conclusions.

During stage one, literature review was conducted using secondary sources as well as a few primary sources, such as reports published by government agencies in Bahrain and the United Nations. This stage helped in identification of the research problem, gaps and questions, and research aim and objectives. Moreover, key factors influencing transformation of government and trust and confidence in government were identified and clarified. Building up on the model developed by Morgeson et al. (2011) and taking into account the factors mentioned above, a conceptual model was developed in stage two. Additionally, the research hypotheses were suggested along with the supporting theories for every defined construct and relationship within the conceptual model.

In stages three and four, research design including research philosophy, research process, methodology and mechanisms for data analysis were identified. In brief, since this research investigates citizens' perspective, the influence of transformation of government on citizens' trust and confidence in government, quantitative methodology was adopted. In doing so, an online survey targeting random ordinary citizens of the Kingdom of Bahrain was developed and distributed. Prior to launching the online survey, a pilot survey was conducted, which involved testing and validating the conceptual model to ensure that the questions were answerable and the collected data was reliable.

As for stage five concerning data analysis, SEM was the chosen multivariate technique, which was found suitable for validating the developed conceptual model. The main purpose behind this was to validate the fitness of the conceptual model and test the hypotheses by performing CFA and path analysis.

Finally, in stage six, the findings from data analysis are discussed, theoretical and practical contributions of this research are presented, limitations and future research directions are highlighted, and the key conclusions are drawn. The associated chapter for each stage is outlined in Fig. 4.1.

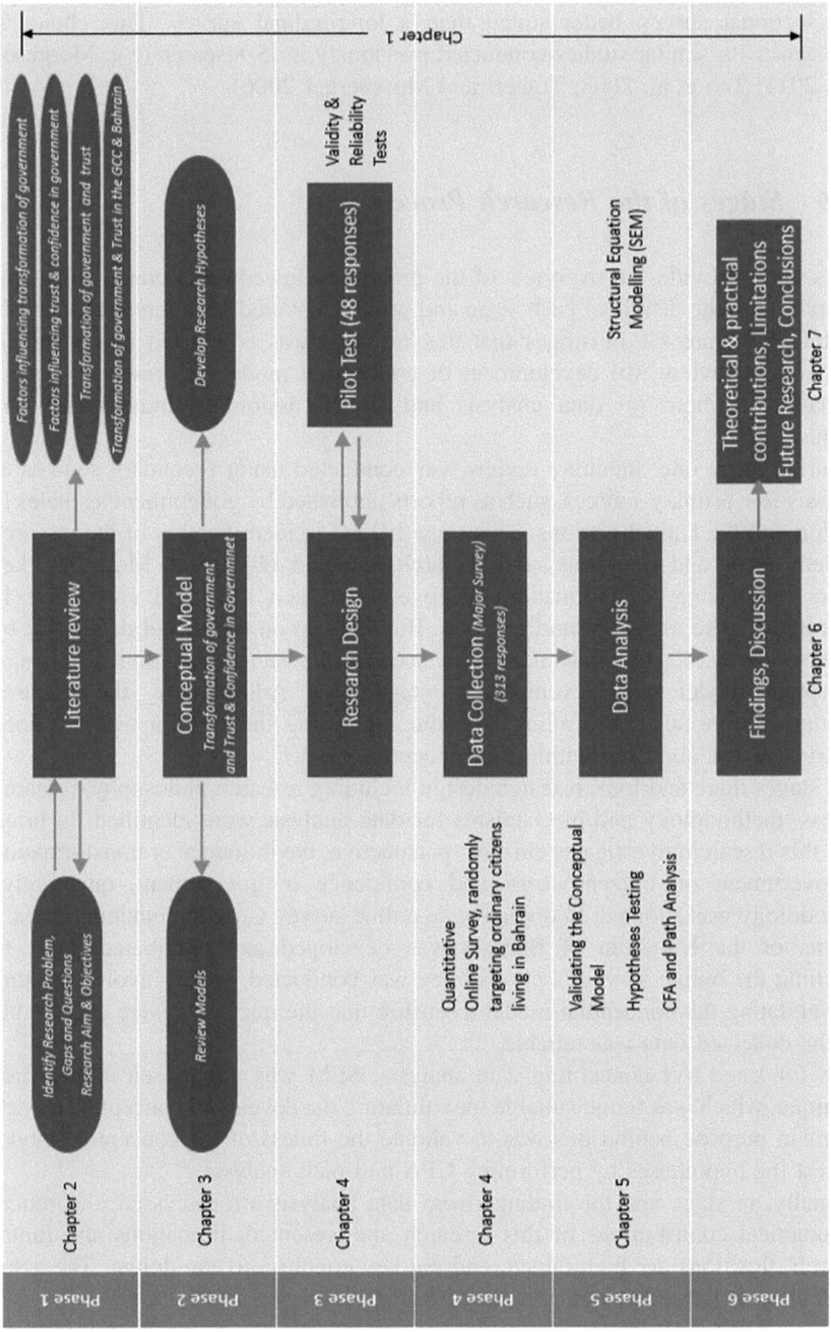

Fig. 4.1 Stages of the research process

4.4 Research Methodology

There are three common methodologies used for conducting research: qualitative, quantitative and mixed method (Bryman and Bell 2007; Creswell 2003). The process of selecting an appropriate research method is based on a number of factors, such as the nature of research, problem to be solved, type of the data needed and accessibility to the data (Punch 2005). A research may use one or more research methods (Punch 2005).

Quantitative method deals with statistics and numbers to explain a phenomenon by normally testing a theory (Creswell 2009; Malhotra and Birks 2007; Zikmund and Babin 2006). It is associated with hypotheses, surveys and questionnaires (Bryman 1992; Denscombe 2003). In IS research, quantitative method is used more frequently than the other two methods. Qualitative method on the other hand, is used to explore and understand a certain phenomenon for developing a theoretical model (Punch 2005; Walsham 2006). Qualitative method is associated with words, explanations, case studies, interviews and observations (Bryman 1992; Denscombe 2003). A number of researchers such as Myers and Avison (1997) pointed out that the qualitative methodology is more effective as it explores in detail the phenomenon that reflects reality. Table 4.1 compares the two methodologies.

The third type is the mixed method approach, which is often called triangulation (Avison et al. 1999; Bryman and Bell 2007; Creswell 2003; Gable 1994; Jick 1979). The purpose of using the mixed method is to use the best of qualitative and

Table 4.1 Comparison between qualitative and quantitative research methodologies

Criteria	Qualitative research	Quantitative research
Purpose	To understand and interpret social interaction	To test hypotheses, look at cause and effect, and make predictions
Group studied	Smaller and not randomly selected	Larger and randomly selected
Type of data collected	Words, images or objects	Specific variables studied
Form of data collected	Open-ended responses, interviews, participant observations, field notes and reflection	Numbers and statistics
Type of data analysis	Identify patterns, features, themes	Data based on precise measurements using structured and validate data-collection instruments
Most common research objectives	Explore, discover and construct	Describe, explain and predict
Focus	Wide-angle lens; examines the breadth and depth of topic	Narrow-angle lens; tests a very specific topic
Results	Findings that are more generalized and directional	Findings that are projectable over population base

Source Adopted from Johnson and Christensen (2008)

quantitative methodologies to understand the problem better (Burns and Bush 2006; Johnson and Onwuegbuzie 2004; Kaplan and Duchon 1988; Venkatesh et al. 2013). In practice, it uses techniques of both methods and the sequence of which method comes first is based on the nature of research problem (Burns and Bush 2006).

As for this research, quantitative research method has been adopted based on a number of reasons, as explained here. This research investigates the influence of transformation of government on citizens' trust and their confidence in government, which is a phenomenon discussed in this research through testing a current theory, validating a developed conceptual model and testing associated hypotheses. This means positivism is the adopted research philosophy, and thus the research seeks citizens' perceptions on all constructs and hypotheses proposed in this research. Since the target audiences for this research are ordinary citizens of the Kingdom of Bahrain, the suitable methodology for capturing a large proportion of the target population is the quantitative method. The use of quantitative methodology in this research is in line with similar studies conducted previously in IS research (e.g. Morgeson et al. 2011; Teo et al. 2008; Tolbert and Mossberger 2006). Qualitative or mixed methodologies are not fitting options for this research, as it would be impractical to use either of them for the reasons explained above.

4.5 Quantitative Method

With the quantitative method, this research uses survey as a mode of observation or data collection technique (for reasons specified in the above sections). It is worth pointing out that survey here refers to a systematic approach for obtaining the needed information from a portion of the targeted audience; findings of the survey are generalized to cover the entire population (Bhattacherjee 2012; Groves et al. 2004). The key components that constitute the survey based approach are explained in the following subsections (Fowler 2002).

4.5.1 Sampling Process

Sampling refers to obtaining the needed data for a research from a percentage of the targeted audience or population (Fowler 2002). It is very important to have the right and appropriate sample so that findings can be generalized to the overall population (Bhattacherjee 2012; Sekaran 2003).

4.5.2 Target Population

Target population can be referred to a target audience or unit of analysis. The target population for this research is citizens (see Sect. 4.3.2).

4.5.3 Sampling Frame

Sampling Frame can be defined as a full list of all units in the population from which the sample is drawn (Bryman and Bell 2007; Churchill and Dawn 1999; Saunders 2011). In this context, the target population or the unit of analysis is citizens, and hence, the sampling frame will comprise of ordinary citizens living in the Kingdom of Bahrain.

4.5.4 Sampling Technique

As per Bhattacherjee (2012) and Saunders (2011), there are two types of sampling techniques, which are probability and non-probability; both types have sub-types (Fig. 4.2). According to the probability sampling technique, all units of sampling frame have the probability of being a part of the sample; non-probability is defined otherwise (Bhattacherjee 2012; Saunders 2011). The selection of appropriate sampling technique is based on the research questions, aim, and objectives; some studies use a combination of different sampling techniques (Bhattacherjee 2012; Saunders 2011).

Since this research captures citizens' perceptions, it adopts probability sampling to ensure that the target audiences have equal opportunity to be included in the study. As for the sub-type of probability sampling, *random sampling* is selected to include as much population in this research. In order to increase the number of

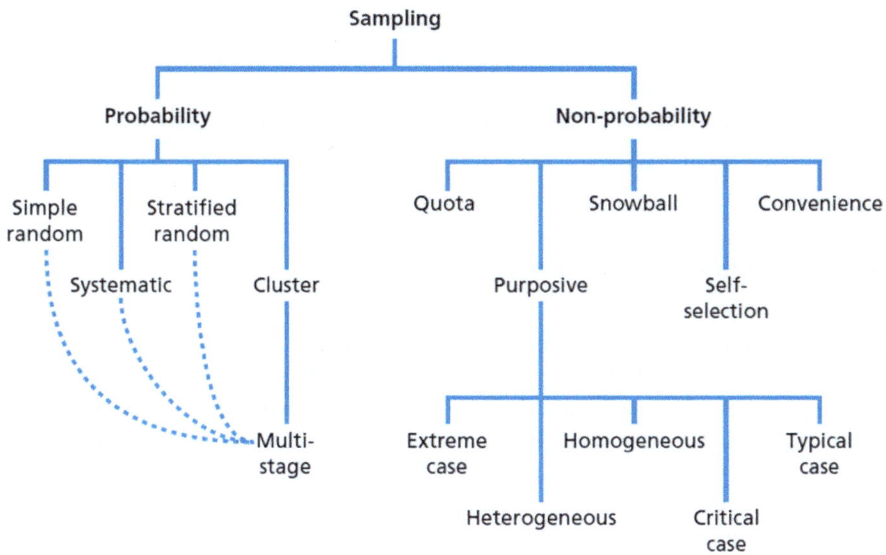

Fig. 4.2 Types of sampling techniques. *Source* Adopted from Saunders (2011)

participants, random sampling is normally used in conjunction with other data collection techniques such as online surveys, postal surveys and/or telephonic surveys (Saunders 2011). Since majority of the citizens in Bahrain are well educated and use Internet regularly, this research uses online random sampling for data collection. Similar researches conducted previously have used the same sampling technique (Dashti et al. 2009; Nam and Sayogo 2011; Weerakkody et al. 2013).

4.5.5 Sample Size

According to the existing literature, there is no definite number agreed by the researchers for a suitable sample size, as it depends on a number of factors (Fowler 2002; Muthen and Muthen 2002). It is preferred to have more samples due to the impact it can have on the accuracy of the results. The sampling size for this research is 313, which is considered as adequate as per Comrey and Lee (1992) and Tabachnick and Fidell (2001).

4.5.6 Data Collection Tool

There are two types of data collection tools: interviews and questionnaires; quantitative methodology often associated with numbers and questionnaires, whereas qualitative method is more to do with words and interviews (Saunders 2011). Since this research adopts a quantitative approach, questionnaires are a suitable data collection tool. Questionnaires contain a number of questions and the target audiences are expected to answer these questionnaires (Bhattacherjee 2012). This research employs a structured questionnaire, as it will allow the citizens participating in the study to select the appropriate answer from the already listed multiple choices.

4.5.7 Types of Questionnaires

Different types of questionnaire are available as shown in Fig. 4.3. Self-administrated questionnaires refer to the prepared questions to be completed by the respondents without any intervention from the researcher (Saunders 2011). The sub-types include internet-mediated questionnaires, postal questionnaires, and delivery and collection questionnaires (Saunders 2011). As opposed to the self-administrated questionnaire, the researcher intervenes while conducting interviewer-administrated questionnaires. For instance, the researcher records respondent's answers. This can be done through telephone or via a face-to-face meeting with the responder (Saunders 2011).

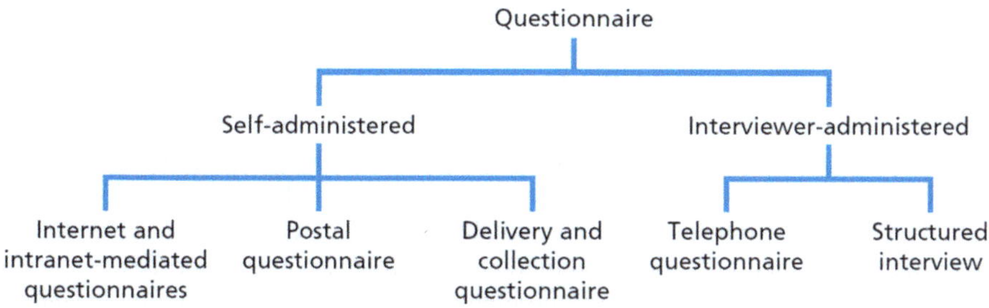

Fig. 4.3 Types of questionnaires. *Source* Adopted from Saunders (2011)

This research employs self-administrated internet-mediated questionnaires, which can be referred to as web-based or online questionnaires. The reason for this selection is based on the fact that majority of citizens in Bahrain are well educated and use Internet regularly. In doing so, a large number of ordinary citizens from different places in the Kingdom of Bahrain as well as variety of backgrounds can be captured. Other reasons for selecting this questionnaire type were related to the time, budget and resource constraints for this research.

The hyperlink to the online questionnaire was distributed to ordinary citizens living in the Kingdom of Bahrain through emails, SMS and social media (i.e. WhatsApp, Facebook and LinkedIn). In order to increase the number of participants in this research, respondents were asked to share the online questionnaire with their contacts. In addition, social media was used to distribute the online questionnaires as it is extensively used by people, and is also regarded as the most powerful distribution tool. The use of social media to distribute the online questionnaires was supported by existing literature (Kayam and Hirsch 2012; Merolli et al. 2014).

4.6 Questionnaire Development and Validation

4.6.1 Overview

Final version of the questionnaire was developed following a number of phases as illustrated in Table 4.2; details of each phase are provided in the subsections. All questions were adopted from previous research (e.g. Abhichandani et al. 2005; Morgeson et al. 2011; Park and Blenkinsopp 2011; Parasuraman et al. 1988).

Table 4.2 Questionnaire development phases

	Phase	Number of questions
1	Pre-pilot test	62
2	Pilot survey	55
3	Main survey	51

The final questionnaire targeting citizens living in the Kingdom of Bahrain comprised of fifty-one close-ended questions and four multiple-choice questions with single answers. The four multiple-choice questions related to demographic variables: gender, age, educational level and income. Taking into account the sensitivity of this research in a small country that is surrounded geographically by many political issues, a 7-point Likert scale was selected for the fifty-one close-ended questions for the purposes of increasing the number of choices and avoiding the selection of the "neutral" choice as much as possible (Bhattacherjee 2012).

The language used in the questionnaire is clear and easy to understand to facilitate ease of completing the questions (Bhattacherjee 2012). Potential respondents were asked to select the best option as they see appropriate based on their perception of all constructs of the conceptual model. The questionnaire refrained from any information related to respondent identity, confirming that the information provided would only be used for the purpose of this research, and will be kept strictly confidential.

For the pilot survey, 71 responses were received, out of which only 48 were found complete. As for the main survey, 513 responses were received, out of which only 313 were found complete. Since majority of the citizens of the Kingdom of Bahrain are well educated and English is the second language of the country, it is used heavily in both public and private sectors. The questionnaire was thus in English and was not translated to Arabic. This selection was confirmed by a number of respondents, who were of different ages as shown in Chap. 5.

4.6.2 Structure of the Questionnaire

This research employed a structured questionnaire with choices to be selected from by the respondents. The questionnaire contained three sections: welcome page, demographic questions and close-ended questions. The welcome page stated the purpose of the questionnaire and the aim and objectives of the research. In addition, the potential respondents were assured of confidentiality. The second section contained four multiple-choice questions with single answers related to the demographic variables: gender, age, educational level and income. The third section contained fifty-one questions with a 7-point Likert scale, covering all nine constructs of the conceptual model. The multiple-choice questions and close-ended 7-point Likert scale questions can be referred to as nominal responses and interval-level responses (Bhattacherjee 2012).

4.6.3 Pre-test

The initial version of the questionnaire consisted of 62 questions adopted from previous research. However, before launching the pilot and main surveys, it was important to conduct a pre-test to ensure that the questionnaire was relevant, not repetitive, easy, clear, and understandable (Burns and Bush 2006; Fowler 2002). For these reasons, two academics (Ph.D. scholars), reviewed the content of the initial questionnaire that resulted in deleting seven questions, editing a few questions and improving the language and grammar for a number of questions.

4.6.4 *Pilot Survey*

Before launching the main survey, a pilot test was carried out in September 2015. Survey Monkey was the website used to publish the online questionnaire. The hyperlink to the survey was communicated via email, SMS and social media applications (WhatsApp, Facebook, and LinkedIn). Table 4.3 illustrates the measuring items for each construct, and the supporting evidence from literature. All 55 questions have been recorded in Appendix A.

Following the distribution of the online survey, a total of 71 responses were received; only 48 responses were considered as complete while the remaining 23 were treated incomplete and not used for analysis purposes. These 48 responses represented a completion rate of 68%, which is an acceptable rate (Baruch 1999; Dommeyer et al. 2002; Ogier 2005). The 68% completion rate could be attributed to the length of the survey, which ran up to 55 questions in total.

Moving to the analysis, validity and reliability tests of the conceptual model was conducted using Statistical Package for the Social Sciences (SPSS) version 23.0. The minimum and maximum values (mentioned below) were derived from literature on research methodology (Robinson et al. 1991; Sekaran 2000). Cronbach's alpha was used to measure the reliability. Alpha values at 0.7 were considered acceptable, exceeding 0.7 were considered good, while those below 0.7 were considered poor (Sekaran 2000). On the other hand, the internal consistency

Table 4.3 Research questions and evidence from the literature

Construct	Measuring items (see Appendix A)	Adopted from
E-Government (EGOV)	Q1–Q10	Abhichandani et al. (2005)
Transparency (TRANSPY)	Q11–Q15	Park and Blenkinsopp (2011)
Accountability (ACOUNT)	Q16–Q20	Said et al. (2015)
Technology (TECH)	Q21–Q23	Hameed and Al-Shawabkah (2013)
Expectation (EXPEC)	Q24–Q36	Parasuraman et al. (1988)
Transformation (TRANSF)	Q37–Q41	Patterson et al. (2005)
Performance (PERFO)	Q42–Q45	Zhang (2013)
Satisfaction (SATISF)	Q46–Q50	Zhang (2013)
Trust and Confidence (TRU_COF)	Q51–Q55	McKnight et al. (2002), Morgeson et al. (2011)

measure was adopted for measuring validity; specifically, inter-item correlation and item to total correlation for each construct were measured. Minimum correlation value was set as acceptable at 0.3, and the maximum was set at 0.8 for inter-item correlation, whereas, minimum correlation value was set as acceptable at 0.5 for item to total correlation (Robinson et al. 1991). Where an item(s) was found to cause concern depending on how close the statistical value of the measure was to the acceptable value, and how many items would remain, if an item(s) were deleted, the criterion to decide whether to retain or delete the item(s) was used to measure a construct (Mahmood and Weerakkody 2016).

Summary of the reliability and validity analyses are shown in Table 4.4. (before deleting any questions). It can be seen that constructs 1 and 5, EGOV and EXPEC, have issues with validity (Table 4.4). Furthermore, constructs 2 and 3, TRANSPY and ACOUNT, have serious issues with both reliability and validity (Table 4.4). Moving forward, removing Q14, Q17, Q29 and Q33 from the main survey resulted in improving the values significantly for reliability and validity (Table 4.5). As for construct 1, EGOV, Q7 was retained for the main survey, as values for Item-to-Item and Item-to-total were expected to change with the larger sample size.

Surprisingly, the five questions mentioned above were the negative questions used in the questionnaire. The main reason for using such questions was to force respondents to consider properly the questions and reduce biases as much as possible. It is believed that respondents may not understood the five negative questions, which resulted in having issues with validly and/or reliability measures of the associated constructs.

After deleting Q14, Q17, Q29 and Q33, reliability and validity tests were conducted again, which resulted in data shown in Table 4.5.

4.6.5 Main Survey

The main survey comprised of 51 questions (see Appendix B and Table 4.6) and was carried out between October 2015 and November 2015 using the same methodology adopted for the pilot study.

It is believed that the hyperlink to the web survey reached around 1000 people living in the Kingdom of Bahrain. In total 513 survey responses were received, out of which only 313 responses were deemed complete. The 513 responses represented a completion rate of 51%, which is considered a good response rate in Information System research (Fowler 2002). As per Comrey and Lee (1992) and Tabachnick and Fidell (2001), the 313 received responses is considered an adequate sampling size.

Despite Q7 for EGOV causing some problems with Item-to-Item and Item-to-total correlations (Sect. 4.6.4), it was retained in the main survey for when the sample size would be increased (Halkett and Kristjanson 2007; Javali et al. 2011). Following the main survey, validity and reliability for EGOV were revisited using the same parameters identified in Sect. 4.6.4 for validity and reliability tests.

Table 4.4 Summary of reliability and validity analyses (before deleting questions)

No.	Construct	Question codes	Cronbach's Alpha	Item-item correlation (range)	Item-total correlation (range)	Remarks
1	EGOV	Q1–Q10	0.817	*−0.328–0.749*	*−0.3–0.725*	Reliability is good, but inter-item and item-to-total correlation are found to range from poor to good, with item Q7 causing some correlation concerns. This item will be retained for the main survey to test its behavior with a larger sample size
2	TRANSPY	Q11–Q15	*0.352*	*−0.519–0.681*	*−0.580–0.605*	Reliability, inter-item correlation and item-to-total correlation are not good, with Q14 causing serious problems. This item will be deleted as it is contributing to significant error to the reliability, inter item correlation and item to total correlation. Reliability, inter-item correlation and item-to-total correlation are unlikely to change even if the sample size is increased
3	ACOUNT	Q16–Q20	*0.617*	*−0.342–0.604*	*−0.084–0.679*	Reliability is poor. Inter-item and item-to-total correlation ranges from poor to good, with item Q17 causing serious problems. This item will be deleted as it is contributing to significant error to the reliability, inter item correlation and item to total correlation. Reliability, inter-item correlation and item-to-total correlation are unlikely to change even if the sample size is increased
4	TECH	Q21–Q23	0.744	0.358–0.629	0.473–0.678	Reliability is good. Inter-item and item-to-total correlation range from acceptable to good. Item-to-total correlation for Q23 is slightly lower than the acceptable level of 0.5 and it is expected to improve with sample size. Hence retained to be part of the main survey questionnaire

(continued)

Table 4.4 (continued)

No.	Construct	Question codes	Cronbach's Alpha	Item-item correlation (range)	Item-total correlation (range)	Remarks
5	EXPEC	Q24–Q36	0.902	*−0.353–0.822*	*0.006–0.859*	Reliability is good, but inter-item and item-to-total correlation values are found to range from poor to good, with items Q29 and Q33 causing some concern with correlation. These items will be deleted as they are unlikely to improve in value even if the sample size is increased
6	TRANSF	Q37–Q41	0.915	0.584–0.816	0.73–0.836	Reliability, inter-item correlation and item-to-total correlation are found to be good. All items will be retained for main survey
7	PERFO	Q41–Q45	0.887	0.558–0.771	0.705 to 0.815	Reliability, inter-item correlation and item-to-total correlation are found to be good. All items will be retained for main survey
8	SATISF	Q46–Q50	0.927	0.429–0.835	0.708–0.907	Reliability, inter-item correlation and item-to-total correlation are found to be good. All items will be retained for main survey
9	TRUST & CONFIDENCE	Q51–Q55	0.903	0.511–0.819	0.659–0.838	Reliability, inter-item correlation and item-to-total correlation are found to be good. All items will be retained for main survey

Table 4.5 Summary of reliability and validity analyses (after deleting Q14, Q17, Q29 and Q33)

No.	Construct	Question codes	Cronbach's Alpha	Item-item correlation (range)	Item-total correlation (range)	Remarks
1	EGOV	Q1–Q10	0.817	*−0.328–0.749*	*−0.3–0.725*	Reliability is good, but inter-item and item-to-total correlations are found to range from poor to good, with item Q7 causing some correlation concerns. This item will be retained for the main survey to test its behavior with a larger sample size
2	TRANSPY	Q11–Q13 Q15	0.816	0.310–0.681	0.520–0.740	After deleting Q14, reliability, inter-item and item-to-total correlations are found to be good
3	ACOUNT	Q16, Q18–Q20	0.778	0.377–0.604	0.499–0.645	Reliability, inter-item and item-to-total correlations are found to be good. All items will be retained except Q17. Deleting Q17 still left four items to measure the construct, and hence causes no concern to the adequacy of the number of items needed to measure a construct
4	TECH	Q21–Q23	0.744	0.358–0.629	0.473–0.678	Reliability value is good. Inter-item and item-to-total correlations range from acceptable to good. Item-to-total correlation for Q23 is slightly lower than the acceptable 0.5, but is expected to improve with sample size. Hence, it is retained in the main survey
5	EXPEC	Q24–Q28, Q30–Q32, Q34–Q36	0.943	0.284–0.822	0.564–0.870	Reliability, inter-item and item-to-total correlations are found to be good. All items will be retained except Q29 and Q33. Even though one correlation value between Q25 and Q30 is showing slightly less than the acceptable value of 0.3 for inter-item correlation, as it is very close to 0.3, it is accepted with the assumption that when sample size increases, correlation will improve. Deleting Q29 and Q33 meant still eleven items were left to measure the construct and hence, there was no cause of concern to the adequacy of the number of items needed to measure a construct

(continued)

Table 4.5 (continued)

No.	Construct	Question codes	Cronbach's Alpha	Item-item correlation (range)	Item-total correlation (range)	Remarks
6	TRANSF	Q37–Q41	0.915	0.584–0.816	0.73–0.836	Reliability, inter-item correlation and item-to-total correlation are found to be good. All items will be retained for main survey
7	PERFO	Q41–Q45	0.887	0.558–0.771	0.705–0.815	Reliability, inter-item correlation and item-to-total correlation are found to be good. All items will be retained for main survey
8	SATISF	Q46–Q50	0.927	0.429–0.835	0.708–0.907	Reliability, inter-item correlation and item-to-total correlation are found to be good. All items will be retained for main survey
9	TRUST & CONFIDENCE	Q51–Q55	0.903	0.511–0.819	0.659–0.838	Reliability, inter-item correlation and item-to-total correlation are found to be good. All items will be retained for main survey

Table 4.6 Main survey—research questions

Construct	Measuring items
EGOV	Q1–Q10
TRANSPY	Q11–Q14
ACOUNT	Q15–Q18
TECH	Q19–Q21
EXPEC	Q22–Q32
TRANSF	Q33–Q37
PERFO	Q38–Q41
SATISF	Q42–Q46
TRU_COF	Q47–Q51

Table 4.7 Summary of the reliability and validity analysis for EGOV (before deleting Q7)

No.	Construct	Question codes	Cronbach's Alpha	Item-item correlation (range)	Item-total correlation (range)	Remarks
1	EGOV	Q1–Q10	0.858	*−0.160–0.725*	*−0.271–0.760*	Reliability is good. However, inter item and item to total correlation are found to range from poor to good, with item Q7 contributing again to this regardless of Increasing the sample size

Table 4.8 Summary of the reliability and validity analysis for EGOV (following deleting Q7)

No.	Construct	Question codes	Cronbach's Alpha	Item-item correlation (range)	Item-total correlation (range)	Remarks
1	EGOV	Q1–Q6, Q8–Q10	0.904	0.312–0.725	0.540–0.760	Reliability and validity values are good following deletion of Q7

Table 4.7 confirms that regardless of the increased sample size, Q7 still caused issues with the validity test. Ultimately, deleting Q7 improved values for validity and reliability (Table 4.8).

Therefore, only the 50 questions listed in Appendix C were considered, and subject to further data analysis (see Chap. 5).

4.7 Data Analysis

Before selecting the suitable data analysis technique, it is important to consider a number of elements such as preparing, inputting and checking the data; this includes the type of data, data layout, coding, entering data and checking for errors (Churchill and Lacobucci 2004; Saunders 2011; Sekaran 2000). The data type used for this research was nominal responses and interval-level responses as highlighted in Sect. 4.6.2. Since this research uses online survey, the other three items, data layout, coding, entering and checking data for errors, were accomplished automatically by the system that run the online survey.

SPSS version 23.0 was used in this research for the data analysis purposes as it is easy to use, flexible, effective in data management, better in organizing output, quick in analyzing data, and includes a number of options such as graphs, charts and modeling (Field 2013; Green and Salkind 2010; Pallant 2013). The data was collected through an online survey by the system that run it and was directly exported to an SPSS file, which did not require any coding of responses and cleaning/checking data for errors. The use of online survey and the system running it saved a lot of time and effort as well as avoided common errors and mistakes made with using a manual approach.

Taking into account the research questions, aim, and objectives, SEM was chosen as a multivariate statistical analysis technique that analyzes structural relationships between variables (Gefen et al. 2000; Hooper et al. 2008; Schreiber et al. 2006; Schumacker and Lomax 2004). In this research, there are variables (Transformation of Government), which act as dependent in one instance and independent on another occasion. Thus, SEM fits properly with the developed conceptual model. Additionally, SEM is used to validate the fitness of the conceptual model, and to test the hypotheses by performing CFA and path analysis (Hair et al. 2006). The tool used for performing CFA and path analysis is Analysis of Moment Structure (AMOS) version 23.0, which is an added SPSS module that includes a graphical interface making it an easy tool for data analysis (Arbuckle and Wothke 1999; Blunch 2012; Byrne 2016). Chapter 5 will elaborate on the data analysis elements of this research.

4.8 Research Ethics

Since this research collected primary data from ordinary citizens living in the Kingdom of Bahrain, it was necessary to obtain an ethics approval before doing so. As per Brunel University's Code of Research Ethics, the ethical approval was obtained (see Appendix E) following successful submission of the application for research ethics approval. The ultimate goal of such ethics approval is to ensure that the research is conducted in a professional and ethical manner whilst respecting rights of the participants.

In the submitted application for research ethics approval, the research problem, questions, aim, and objectives were mentioned, along with details of research methodology, target audience, sampling technique, data collection tool, type of questionnaire and mode of questionnaire distribution in the Kingdom of Bahrain.

4.9 Summary

This chapter provides an overview of the suitable methodology and related research techniques adopted for this research. It starts with justifying the reasons for selecting positivist research philosophy compared to interpretive and critical research. Then, it moves to the research purpose where justifications are outlined for the selection of explanatory research. The research process across six phases is then explained. As for research methodology, the reasons for selecting quantitative approach are identified. Justifications for the use of online survey are provided. Different elements of the sampling process such as target population, sampling frame, sampling technique and sampling size are also discussed.

The structure and other elements of the questionnaire as well as the process followed for questionnaire development and validation are highlighted, including information on pre-test, pilot test and the main survey. Justifications for the selection of SEM and AMOS for data analysis are also offered. The chapter concludes with information on research ethics approval that was successfully obtained prior to data collection. The next chapter presents the data analysis process and findings from CFA and path analysis.

References

Abhichandani T, Horan TA, Rayalu R (2005) EGOVSAT: toward a robust measure of e-government service satisfaction in transportation. In: Remenyi D (ed) Proceedings of the International Conference on E-Government (ICEG 2005). Curran Associates, Inc., Red Hook, pp 1–12

Arbuckle JL, Wothke W (1999) Amos 4.0 user's guide. SmallWaters Corporation, Chicago, pp 1995–2005

Avison DE, Lau F, Myers MD, Nielsen PA (1999) Action research. Commun ACM 42(1):94–97

Baruch Y (1999) Response rate in academic studies—a comparative analysis. Hum Relat 52 (4):421–438

Bhattacherjee A (2012) Social science research: principles, methods, and practices

Blunch, N. (2012) Introduction to structural equation modeling using IBM SPSS statistics and AMOS. Sage

Bryman A. (1992) Quantitative and qualitative research: further reflections on their integration. Mixing Methods: Qual Quant Res 57–78

Bryman A (2004) Social research methods, 2nd edn. Oxford University Press, Oxford

Bryman A, Bell E (2007) Business research methods, 2nd edn. Oxford University Press

Burns AC, Bush RF (2006) Marketing research. Globalization 1:7

Byrne BM (2016) Structural equation modeling with AMOS: basic concepts, applications, and programming. Routledge

Chen W, Hirschheim R (2004) A paradigmatic and methodological examination of information systems research from 1991 to 2001. Inf Syst J 14(3):197–235

Churchill GA, Dawn I (1999) Marketing research: methodological foundations. Cengage Learning, vol 9

Churchill GA, Lacobucci D (2004) Marketing research: methodological foundations, 9th edn. Thomson South-Western, Ohio

Collis J, Hussey R (2003) Business research: a practical guide for undergraduate and postgraduate students, 2nd edn. Palgrave Macmillan

Comrey A, Lee H (1992) A first course in factor analysis. Lawrence Erlbaum Associates, Hillsdale

Creswell JW (2003) Research design: quantitative, qualitative, and mixed methods approaches. Sage Publication Inc., Thousand Oaks

Creswell JW (2009) Research design: qualitative, quantitative, and mixed methods approaches. SAGE Publications. Incorporated

Dashti A, Benbasat I, Burton-Jones A (2009) Developing trust reciprocity in electronic-government: the role of felt trust. In: Proceedings of the European and Mediterranean Conference on Information Systems, Izmir, Turkey, pp 1–13

Denscombe, M. (2003) The good research guide Maidenhead

Field A (2013) Discovering statistics using IBM SPSS statistics. Sage

Fowler FJ Jr (2002) Survey research methods. Sage Publications Inc., London

Gable GG (1994) Integrating case study and survey research methods: an example in information systems. Eur J Inf Syst 3(2):112–126

Gefen D, Straub D, Boudreau MC (2000) Structural equation modeling and regression: guidelines for research practice. Commun Assoc Inf Syst 4(1):7

Green SB, Salkind NJ (2010) Using SPSS for Windows and Macintosh: analyzing and understanding data. Prentice Hall Press

Gregor S (2006) The nature of theory in information systems. MIS Q 611–642

Groves RM, Fowler FJ Jr, Couper MP (2004) Survey methodology. Wiley-IEEE

Guba EG, Lincoln YS (1994) Competing paradigms in qualitative research. Handb Qual Res 2:163–194

Hair JF, Tatham RL, Anderson RE, Black W (2006) Multivariate data analysis. Pearson Prentice Hall, Upper Saddle River

Halkett GK, Kristjanson LJ (2007) Validity and reliability testing of two instruments to measure breast cancer patients' concerns and information needs relating to radiation therapy. Radiat Oncol 2(1):43

Hameed S, Al-Shawabkah A (2013) Role of e-government in improving organizational performance in the civil status and passports department of Jordan. Dev Country Stud 3 (5):50–64

Hooper D, Coughlan J, Mullen M (2008) Structural equation modelling: guidelines for determining model fit. Articles p 2

Howe KR (1988) Against the quantitative-qualitative incompatibility thesis or dogmas die hard. Educ Res 17(8):10–16

Javali SB, Gudaganavar NV, Raj SM (2011) Effect of varying sample size in estimation of coefficients of internal consistency

Jick TD (1979) Mixing qualitative and quantitative methods: triangulation in action. Adm Sci Q 24 (4):602–611

Johnson B, Christensen L (2008) Educational research: quantitative, qualitative, and mixed approaches. Sage

Johnson RB, Onwuegbuzie AJ (2004) Mixed methods research: a research paradigm whose time has come. Educ Res 33(7):14–26

Kaplan B, Duchon D (1988) Combining qualitative and quantitative methods in information systems research: a case study. MIS Q 571–586

Kayam O, Hirsch T (2012) Using social media networks to conduct questionnaire based research in social studies case study: family language policy. J Sociol Res 3(2):57–67
Mahmood M, Weerakkody V (2016) Factors affecting citizens' trust and confidence in government and its relation with transformation of government. In: 22nd Americas Conference on Information Systems
Malhotra N, Birks D (2007) Marketing Research: an applied approach, 3rd edn. European Edition, Pearson Education
Myers MD, Avison D (1997) Qualitative research in information systems. Manage Inf SystQ (21):241–242
McKnight DH, Choudhury V, Kacmar C (2002) Developing and validating trust measures for e-commerce: an integrative typology. Inf Syst Res 13(3):334–359
Merolli M, Sanchez FJM, Gray K (2014) Social media and online survey: tools for knowledge management in health research. In: Proceedings of the Seventh Australasian Workshop on Health Informatics and Knowledge Management, vol 153. Australian Computer Society, Inc., pp 21–29
Mingers J (2001) Combining IS research methods: towards a pluralist methodology. Inf Syst Res 12(3):240–259
Mingers J (2003) The paucity of multi-method research: a review of the information systems literature. Inf Syst J 13(3):233–249
Morgeson FV, VanAmburg D, Mithas S (2011) Misplaced trust? Exploring the structure of the e-government-citizen trust relationship. J Public Adm Res Theor 21(2):257–283
Muthen LK, Muthen BO (2002) How to use a Monte Carlo study to decide on sample size and determine power. Struct Equ Model 9(4):599–620
Nam T, Sayogo DS (2011) Who uses e-government?: examining the digital divide in e-government use. In: Proceedings of the 5th International Conference on Theory and Practice of Electronic Governance. ACM, pp 27–36
Niehaves B, Bernd CS (2006) Criticality, epistemology and behaviour vs. design-information systems researchacross different sets of paradigms. Proceedings of the 14th European Conference on Information Systems, AIS
Ogier J (2005) The response rates for online surveys—a hit and miss affair. In: 2005 Australasian Evaluations Forum: University Learning and Teaching: Evaluating and Enhancing the Experience, UNSW, Sydney, 28–29 November
Orlikowski WJ, Baroudi JJ (1991) Studying information technology in organizations: research approaches and assumptions. Inf Syst Res 2(1):1–28
Pallant J (2013) SPSS survival manual. McGraw-Hill Education, UK
Parasuraman A, Zeithaml Valerie A, Berry Leonard L (1988) SERVQUAL: a multiple-item scale for measuring consumer perceptions of service quality. J Retail 64(1):12–40
Park H, Blenkinsopp J (2011) The roles of transparency and trust in the relationship between corruption and citizen satisfaction. Int Rev Admin Sci 77(2):254–274
Patterson MG, West MA, Shackleton VJ, Dawson JF, Lawthom R, Maitlis S, Wallace AM (2005) Validating the organizational climate measure: links to managerial practices, productivity and innovation. J Organ Behav 26(4):379–408
Punch K (2005) Introduction to social research: quantitative and qualitative approaches, 2nd edn. Sage, London
Richardson H, Robinson B (2007) The mysterious case of the missing paradigm: a review of critical information systems research 1991–2001. Inf Syst J 17(3):251–270
Robinson JP, Shaver PR, Wrightsman LS (1991) Criteria for scale selection and evaluation. Meas Pers Soc Psychol Attitudes 1(3):1–16
Robson C (2002) Real word research. Blackwell, Oxford
Said IA, Iaafar NH, Atan R (2015) Assessing accountability in government linked companies: an empirical evidence. Int Bus Manage 9(4):460–469
Saunders MN (2011) Research methods for business students, 5th edn. Pearson Education India
Saunders MN, Saunders M, Lewis P, Thornhill A (2011) Research methods for business students, 5th edn. Pearson Education India

Schreiber JB, Nora A, Stage FK, Barlow EA, King J (2006) Reporting structural equation modelling and confirmatory factor analysis results: a review. J Educ Res 99(6):323–338
Schumacker RE, Lomax RG (2004) A beginner's guide to structural equation modeling. Psychology Press
Sekaran U (2000) Research methods for business: a skill-building approach. Wiley, USA
Sekaran U (2003) Research methods for business: a skill building approach, 4th edn. Wiley, New York
Straub D, Boudreau MC, Gefen D (2004) Validation guidelines for IS positivist research. Commun Assoc Inf Syst 13:380–427
Tabachnick BG, Fidell LS, Osterlind SJ (2001) Using multivariate statistics. Pearson, New York
Teo TS, Srivastava SC, Jiang L (2008) Trust and electronic government success: an empirical study. J Manage Inf Syst 25(3):99–132
Tolbert CJ, Mossberger K (2006) The effects of e-government on trust and confidence in government. Public Adm Rev 66(3):354–369
Venkatesh V, Brown SA, Bala H (2013) Bridging the qualitative-quantitative
Walsham G (1995) Interpretive case studies in IS research: nature and method. Eur J Inf Syst 4:74–81
Walsham G (2006) Doing interpretive research. Eur J Inf Syst 15(3):320–330
Weber R (2004) The rhetoric of positivism versus interpretivism: a personal view. MIS Q 28(1): iii–xii
Weerakkody V, El-Haddadeh R, Al-Sobhi F, Shareef MA, Dwivedi YK (2013) Examining the influence of intermediaries in facilitating e-government adoption: an empirical investigation. Int J Inf Manage 33(5):716–725
Yin RK (2003) Applications of case study research. SAGE, Newbury Park
Yin RK (2009) Case study research: design and methods. Sage Publications, Inc.
Zhang, J. (2013) Towards a citizen-centered e-government: exploring citizens' satisfaction with e-government in China. Doctoral dissertation, Northern Illinois University. Available from ProQuest: https://search.proquest.com/openview/779b13a52e70b97e56b8e9f3c7f4419c/1?pq-origsite=gscholar&cbl=18750&diss=y
Zikmund W, Babin B (2006) Exploring marketing research. Cengage Learning

Chapter 5
Data Analysis

5.1 Introduction

Chapter 4 covered the research design, including research philosophy, research process, methodology and mechanisms for data analysis. The chapter uses quantitative research method by distributing an online survey to the citizens of Kingdom of Bahrain for investigating the influence of transformation of government on citizens' trust and confidence in government. It also presents findings from the different tests performed on the collected data.

Taking into account the research methodology explained in Chap. 4, SEM was chosen as the multivariate technique to validate the fitness of the proposed conceptual model. Before performing CFA and path analysis, a number of tests were conducted to clean the data, which included Exploratory Factor Analysis (EFA), reliability and validity of the research instrument, correlation and normality of the data distribution.

This chapter is structured as follows. Sections 5.2 and 5.3 present response rate and profile of the respondents, respectively. Results of EFA are presented in Sect. 5.4, and validity and reliability of research instrument is covered in Sect. 5.5. Descriptive statistics are presented in Sect. 5.6. Correlation and normality assessments are included in Sects. 5.7 and 5.8, respectively. Analyses conducted under SEM, including CFA and path analysis, are presented in Sects. 5.9, 5.10 and 5.11, respectively. Mediation effects including total, direct and indirect effects are included in Sect. 5.12. Section 5.13 then summarizes the chapter.

5.2 Response Rate and Sampling Size

This research uses an online survey comprising of 51 questions that was distributed between October 2015 and November 2015 using email, SMS and social media to the citizens of the Kingdom of Bahrain. Of the total 513 received responses, only

M. Mahmood, *Does Digital Transformation of Government Lead to Enhanced Citizens' Trust and Confidence in Government?*, Springer Theses,
https://doi.org/10.1007/978-3-030-01759-0_5

313 were complete and usable for this research. In dealing with missing values, mean was used as a substitution (Pigott 2001). However, the use of mean created problems with the normality tests [Skewness & Kurtosis, Kolmogorov-Smirnov (K-S) and Shapiro-Wilk (S-W)] and values of the correlation matrix. To fix this problem, all 200 responses with missing values were discarded (Pigott 2001). Therefore, the total number of responses considered in this research was 313 that resulted in achieving better values for normality tests and correlation matrix. Additionally, the fitness of the model and validity results also improved.

Taking into account the researchers' wide network of contacts in the Kingdom of Bahrain, it is believed that the online web survey reached about 1000 people altogether. Thus, the response rate in this case is 51%, which is considered a good response rate in Information System research (Fowler 2002). As per Comrey and Lee (1992) and Tabachnich and Fidell (2001), the 313 received responses is considered as an adequate sampling size.

5.3 Respondent Profile

The online survey included demographic questions such as gender, age, educational level and income. The profile of respondents is illustrated in Table 5.1, which confirms that no significant gender or age bias was present. As for education level and income, it can be noticed that a large proportion of the respondents were highly educated and well paid.

5.4 Factor Analysis

Factor analysis is a statistical method used to verify construct validity and to explain correlation between variables; it can be conducted using EFA and CFA. Practically, it groups variables based on significant correlation (Henson and Roberts 2006; Thompson 2004; Williams et al. 2010). According to the existing literature, EFA can be used followed by CFA for the purpose of identifying potential problems with variables early in the process, and thus preparing variables for a cleaner SEM phase (Cabrera-Nguyen 2010; Worthington and Whittaker 2006). This research thus uses EFA to spot early in the process any potential problems with the variables, so that CFA using SEM can be conducted smoothly.

About 50 questions as listed in Appendix C were identified in Chap. 4, which were to be subject to data analysis. After running the factor analysis in SPSS 23.0, three questions (Q7, Q8 and Q9) out of the nine for the EGOV construct were eliminated as they were loading on a different factor. Apart from the above, factor analysis results were satisfactory. Accordingly, the final number of questions is 47, as listed in Appendix D.

Table 5.1 Profile of the respondents

Gender	Frequency (%)	Age	Frequency (%)	Education	Frequency (%)	Income	Frequency (%)
Male	195 (62.3)	<18	3 (1.0)	Less than secondary school	0 (0)	Under US$500	78 (24.9)
Female	118 (37.7)	18–30	142 (45.4)	Secondary school	11 (3.5)	US$500 to US$1000	22 (7)
		31–40	90 (28.8)	Diploma	22 (7.0)	US$1000 to US$1500	21 (6.7)
		41–50	45 (14.4)	Bachelor's degree	184 (58.8)	US$1500 to US$2000	22 (7)
		>50	33 (10.5)	Master's degree	96 (30.7)	More than US$2000	170 (54.4)
Total	313						

Table 5.2 Values for reliability and validity assessment

	Measuring tool	Recommended value	References
Reliability	Cronbach's alpha	Value = 0.7: Acceptable Value > 0.7: Good Value < 0.7: Poor	(Sekaran 2000)
Validity	Inter-item correlation	Minimum = 0.3 Maximum = 0.8	(Robinson et al. 1991)
	Item to total correlation	Maximum = 0.5	

5.5 Reliability and Validity Analysis

In order to ensure the consistency and accuracy of this research, it is essential to conduct reliability and validity tests of the research instrument. Minimum and maximum values proposed for both reliability and validity are illustrated in Table 5.2 (see Sect. 4.6.4).

Results of the reliability and validity analyses carried out on the 47 questions are shown in Table 5.3 below. The values of Cronbach's alpha, Inter-item correlation and Item-to total correlation are exceeding 0.7, 0.3 and 0.5, respectively. Therefore, it can be concluded that the research instrument is valid and reliable.

5.6 Descriptive Statistics

Table 5.4 presents the mean and standard deviation for all items of the nine constructs included in this research. In this table, the 47 questions are coded to clearly link each question with its construct. Moreover, the coding helps in organizing the data and assists in the analysis phase.

Values for mean ranged from 3.39 to 4.56 (where 1 = minimum, and 7 = maximum), which indicate that responses were between neither disagree nor agree to agree. This means that the respondents were not very impressed with the government services provided in the Kingdom of Bahrain. The respondents showed agreement for all items of e-government, technology, performance, satisfaction, and trust and confidence. On the other hand, they showed less agreement with items of transparency, accountability, citizen expectations and transformation of government.

5.7 Correlation Matrix

In order to describe the degree of relationships between the variables of this research, a correlation matrix is used. Table 5.5 presents the correlation matrix, which also includes the mean and standard deviation. It is clear from Table 5.5 that there is significant correlation (Bartko 1966; Lee Rodgers and Nicewander 1988; Taylor 1990) amongst the variables, with the values ranging from 0.566 to 0.860.

Table 5.3 Reliability and validity assessment

No.	Construct	Question #	# Items	N	Cronbach's alpha	Item-item correlation (range)	Item-total correlation (range)	Remarks
1	EGOV	Q1–Q6	6	313	0.892	0.425–0.733	0.573–0.803	Reliability, inter item correlation and item to total correlation are good
2	TRANSPY	Q11–Q13	4	313	0.844	0.501–0.620	0.629–0.705	Reliability, inter item correlation and item to total correlation are good
3	ACOUNT	Q14–Q17	4	313	0.861	0.535–0.695	0.644–0.768	Reliability, inter item correlation and item to total correlation are good
4	TECH	Q18–Q20	3	313	0.793	0.532–0.589	0.616–9.658	Reliability, inter item correlation and item to total correlation are good
5	EXPEC	Q21–Q31	11	313	0.946	0.551–0.761	0.712–0.798	Reliability, inter item correlation and item to total correlation are good
6	TRANSF	Q32–Q36	5	313	0.927	0.640–0.779	0.756–827	Reliability, inter item correlation and item to total correlation are good
7	PERFO	Q37–Q40	4	313	0.899	0.629–0.742	0.733–0.793	Reliability, inter item correlation and item to total correlation are good
8	SATISF	Q41–Q45	5	313	0.932	0.657–0.785	0.787–0.837	Reliability, inter item correlation and item to total correlation are good
9	TRUST & CONFIDENCE	Q46–Q50	5	313	0.934	0.679–0.832	0.757–0.864	Reliability, inter item correlation and item to total correlation are good

Legend N = Sample size

Table 5.4 Descriptive statistics

Construct	Item	Code	N	Mean	Std. deviation
EGOV	Q1	EGOV1	313	4.3479	1.55301
	Q2	EGOV2	313	4.4335	1.51929
	Q3	EGOV3	313	4.4045	1.48574
	Q4	EGOV4	313	4.0668	1.49645
	Q5	EGOV5	313	4.1229	1.47682
	Q6	EGOV6	313	4.0369	1.55930
TRANSPY	Q7	TRANSPY1	313	3.8875	1.43689
	Q8	TRANSPY2	313	3.6497	1.48583
	Q9	TRANSPY3	313	3.6126	1.62085
	Q10	TRANSPY4	313	4.0077	1.40967
ACOUNT	Q11	ACOUNT1	313	4.1132	1.48731
	Q12	ACOUNT2	313	3.8680	1.56146
	Q13	ACOUNT3	313	3.8883	1.45463
	Q14	ACOUNT4	313	3.6598	1.46090
TECH	Q15	TECH1	313	4.2480	1.58759
	Q16	TECH2	313	4.5605	1.48544
	Q17	TECH3	313	4.0329	1.58283
EXPEC	Q18	EXPEC1	313	3.8442	1.50819
	Q19	EXPEC2	313	3.8777	1.59373
	Q20	EXPEC3	313	3.6391	1.55421
	Q21	EXPEC4	313	3.9777	1.50304
	Q22	EXPEC5	313	3.8983	1.49767
	Q23	EXPEC6	313	3.7913	1.48265
	Q24	EXPEC7	313	3.9138	1.47170
	Q25	EXPEC8	313	4.3646	1.54830
	Q26	EXPEC9	313	3.9770	1.50729
	Q27	EXPEC10	313	3.7247	1.58133
	Q28	EXPEC11	313	3.7581	1.59462
TRANSF	Q29	TRANSF1	313	3.5756	1.55843
	Q30	TRANSF2	313	3.6028	1.58955
	Q31	TRANSF3	313	3.4431	1.53438
	Q32	TRANSF4	313	3.3967	1.60360
	Q33	TRANSF5	313	3.6119	1.61094
PERFO	Q34	PERFO1	313	4.0995	1.52440
	Q35	PERFO2	313	4.2621	1.52997
	Q36	PERFO3	313	4.0332	1.48677
	Q37	PERFO4	313	4.2323	1.50616
SATISF	Q38	SATISF1	313	4.2624	1.52998
	Q39	SATISF2	313	4.3084	1.51315
	Q40	SATISF3	313	4.2522	1.50520
	Q41	SATISF4	313	4.3521	1.47718
	Q42	SATISF5	313	4.4011	1.48337

(continued)

Table 5.4 (continued)

Construct	Item	Code	N	Mean	Std. deviation
TRU_COF	Q43	TRU_COF1	313	4.1527	1.54318
	Q44	TRU_COF2	313	4.1094	1.52058
	Q45	TRU_COF3	313	4.0762	1.60653
	Q46	TRU_COF4	313	4.0261	1.58295
	Q47	TRU_COF5	313	4.2579	1.62695

5.8 Normality of the Data

In order to validate the normality of the data distribution, skewness and kurtosis test was performed (Hair et al. 2006). Skewness refers to the symmetry of the distribution, while Kurtosis refers to the degree to which the data distribution is peaked (Pallant 2010). The parameters for measuring skewness and kurtosis are illustrated in Table 5.6.

Table 5.7 illustrates results from the skewness and kurtosis test, which indicates that no item skewness exceeded ±1.5 and no kurtosis value exceeded ±3.0. As such, the distribution of data is considered normal.

5.9 Structural Equation Modelling

This research adopts SEM as the multivariate statistical analysis technique that combines EFA and multiple regression. It analyzes the structural relationships between variables included in this research through performing CFA and path analysis (Hair et al. 2006). SEM has two models, the measurement model, and the structural model; the measurement model investigates the relationships between observed (measured) and latent variables, whereas the structural model investigates the relationships between latent variables only (Suhr 2006).

5.10 Confirmatory Factor Analysis

5.10.1 Measurement Model Fit

CFA was conducted using AMOS to test the measurement model. Before presenting the results of CFA, it is important to point out that the model fit is measured using a number of fit indices such as Chi-square, Goodness of Fit Index (GFI), Degree of Freedom (DF), Comparative Fit Index (CFI), Normed Fit Index (NFI),

Table 5.5 Mean, Std. Deviation and Correlation

	Mean	Std. deviation	EGOV	TRANSPY	ACOUNT	TECH	EXPEC	TRANSF	PERFO
EGOV	37.0224	10.66008							
TRANSPY	15.2115	4.9846	0.786**						
ACOUNT	15.609	5.07264	0.744**	0.761**					
TECH	12.8494	3.95403	0.707**	0.698**	0.758**				
EXPEC	42.8109	13.61511	0.731**	0.748**	0.794**	0.748**			
TRANSF	17.5641	7.02849	0.566**	0.678**	0.691**	0.587**	0.787**		
PERFO	16.6603	5.35652	0.722**	0.691**	0.689**	0.672**	0.756**	0.602**	
SATISF	21.6667	6.7338	0.709**	0.670**	0.662**	0.667**	0.759**	0.553**	0.860**

Note $*p < 0.05$, $**p < 0.01$, $***p < 0.001$

Table 5.6 Parameters for skewness and kurtosis

	Positive form	Negative form	Acceptable range	References
Skewness	Distribution is shifted to the left	Distribution is shifted to the right	+1.5 to −1.5	Li (1999), Pallant (2010)
Kurtosis	Flat distribution of data	Peaked distribution of data	+3 to −3	Li (1999), Pallant (2010)

Table 5.7 Results of skewness and kurtosis test

	N	Mean	Std. deviation	Skewness		Kurtosis	
	Statistic	Statistic	Statistic	Statistic	Std. error	Statistic	Std. error
EGOV Q1–Q6	313	37.0224	10.66008	−0.047	0.138	−0.575	0.275
TRANSPY Q10–Q13	313	15.2115	4.98460	0.207	0.138	−0.292	0.275
ACOUNT Q14–Q17	313	15.6090	5.07264	−0.020	0.138	−0.416	0.275
TECH Q18–Q20	313	12.8494	3.95403	−0.031	0.138	−0.318	0.275
EXPEC Q21–Q31	313	42.8109	13.61511	0.053	0.138	−0.268	0.275
TRANSF Q32–Q36	313	17.5641	7.02849	0.156	0.138	−0.643	0.275
PERFO Q37–Q40	313	16.6603	5.35652	−0.113	0.138	−0.484	0.275
SATISF Q41–Q45	313	21.6667	6.73380	−0.182	0.138	−0.348	0.275
Valid N (listwise)	313						

Incremental Fit Index (IFI), Relative Fit Index (RFI), Tucker-Lewis Index (TLI), Root Mean Square Residual (RMR) and Root Mean Square Error of Approximation (RMSEA) (Schreiber et al. 2006; Hair et al. 2006). However, there is no common set of agreed fit indices to be reported (Jackson et al. 2009) and the same applies to the acceptable values for fit indices (Hair et al. 2006; Schreiber et al. 2006).

This research reports seven fit indices as listed in Table 5.8, which have been often reported at many instances by different studies (Hooper 2008; Iacobucci 2010).

Performing CFA resulted in the following values for CMIN/DF, RMSEA, TLI, CFI and IFI (Table 5.9), which were found to be in line with the recommended values. Furthermore, GFI at 0.786 was very close to the recommended value of 0.8, but RMR at 0.101 did not meet its recommended value of 0.05.

Of the seven fit indices suggested, five fit indices were found acceptable and one that is GFI was very close to the acceptable value. Therefore, CFA for the proposed model resulted in a good fit.

Table 5.8 Recommended levels for fit indices

Fit indices	Recommended value	References
Chi-square test statistic CMIN/df	1.00–3.00	Lee et al. (2015)
Goodness-of fit index (GFI)	>0.80	Lee et al. (2015)
Root mean square error of app. (RMSEA)	<0.08	Lee et al. (2015)
Root mean squared residual (RMR)	<0.05	Lee et al. (2015)
Tucker-Lewis Index (TLI)	>0.90	Hu and Bentler (1999)
Comparative Fit Index (CFI)	>0.90	Hu and Bentler (1999)
Incremental Fit Index (IFI)	>0.90	Hu and Bentler (1999)

Table 5.9 Values for fit indices

Fit indices	Recommended value	Structural model
Chi-square test statistic ($\chi 2$)/df	1.00–3.00	1997.084/991 = 2.015
Goodness-of fit index (GFI)	>0.80	0.786
Root mean square error of app. (RMSEA)	<0.08	0.057
Root mean squared residual (RMR)	<0.05	0.101
Tucker-Lewis Index (TLI)	>0.90	0.916
Comparative Fit Index (CFI)	>0.90	0.923
Incremental Fit Index (IFI)	>0.90	0.923

Table 5.10 Recommended values for standardized loadings, C.R, SMC

Parameters	Recommended value	References
Standardized loadings	>0.5	Hair et al. (2010)
Critical Rations (C.R)	> ±1.96 ($p < 0.001$)	Hox and Bechger (1998)
R square (SMC)	<=0.9	Field (2006), Tabachnich and Fidell (2011)

5.10.2 Standardized Loadings, Critical Ratios and R Squares

The next step is to present standardized loadings, Critical Ratios (CR) and R Square (Squared Multiple Correlations, SMC) for all items of the measurement model. The acceptable values for each are illustrated in Table 5.10.

As shown in Table 5.11, all values of standardized loadings (Standardized Regression Weights, S.R.W) are greater than 0.5. The C.R. values are above ±1.96 ($p < 0.001$). As for the SMC values, all values are below 0.9.

Based on the above results, construct validity can be assessed. Before doing so, the measurement model is presented below (Figure 5.1).

Table 5.11 Values for Standardized loadings, C.R, SMC

Structural relation			R.W.	S.E.	C.R.	S.R.W	SMC
ACOUNT1	←	cACOUNT	1.204	0.071	17.035	0.811	0.657
ACOUNT2	←	cACOUNT	1.253	0.075	16.819	0.804	0.646
ACOUNT3	←	cACOUNT	1.15	0.07	16.447	0.792	0.627
ACOUNT4	←	cACOUNT	1.039	0.073	14.174	0.713	0.508
EGOV1	←	cEGOV	0.927	0.083	11.199	0.598	0.357
EGOV2	←	cEGOV	1.294	0.07	18.455	0.853	0.728
EGOV3	←	cEGOV	1.197	0.071	16.768	0.808	0.653
EGOV4	←	cEGOV	1.166	0.072	16.115	0.781	0.609
EGOV5	←	cEGOV	1.202	0.071	17.042	0.815	0.664
EGOV6	←	cEGOV	1.156	0.077	14.999	0.742	0.551
EXPEC1	←	cEXPEC	1.162	0.072	16.047	0.772	0.596
EXPEC10	←	cEXPEC	1.232	0.076	16.301	0.781	0.609
EXPEC11	←	cEXPEC	1.255	0.076	16.544	0.789	0.622
EXPEC2	←	cEXPEC	1.249	0.076	16.455	0.785	0.616
EXPEC3	←	cEXPEC	1.182	0.075	15.747	0.762	0.58
EXPEC4	←	cEXPEC	1.167	0.072	16.235	0.778	0.605
EXPEC5	←	cEXPEC	1.203	0.071	17.06	0.804	0.647
EXPEC6	←	cEXPEC	1.215	0.069	17.579	0.821	0.673
EXPEC7	←	cEXPEC	1.19	0.069	17.242	0.81	0.656
EXPEC8	←	cEXPEC	1.144	0.076	15.113	0.74	0.547
EXPEC9	←	cEXPEC	1.162	0.072	16.04	0.772	0.596
PERFO1	←	cPERFO	1.263	0.071	17.761	0.83	0.688
PERFO2	←	cPERFO	1.294	0.071	18.345	0.847	0.717
PERFO3	←	cPERFO	1.166	0.071	16.359	0.786	0.617
PERFO4	←	cPERFO	1.293	0.069	18.788	0.86	0.739
SATISF1	←	cSATISF	1.341	0.069	19.55	0.878	0.771
SATISF2	←	cSATISF	1.318	0.068	19.335	0.872	0.761
SATISF3	←	cSATISF	1.278	0.069	18.543	0.85	0.723
SATISF4	←	cSATISF	1.186	0.07	17.007	0.804	0.646
SATISF5	←	cSATISF	1.294	0.067	19.389	0.874	0.764
TECH1	←	cTECH	1.122	0.082	13.68	0.708	0.501
TECH2	←	cTECH	1.011	0.078	13.026	0.681	0.464
TECH3	←	cTECH	1.249	0.079	15.884	0.79	0.624
TRANSF1	←	cTRANSF	1.265	0.074	17.191	0.813	0.661
TRANSF2	←	cTRANSF	1.397	0.072	19.498	0.88	0.775
TRANSF3	←	cTRANSF	1.314	0.07	18.693	0.858	0.736
TRANSF4	←	cTRANSF	1.343	0.075	17.988	0.839	0.703
TRANSF5	←	cTRANSF	1.327	0.076	17.527	0.825	0.681
TRANSPY1	←	cTRANSPY	1.134	0.07	16.254	0.79	0.625
TRANSPY2	←	cTRANSPY	1.09	0.074	14.648	0.735	0.54

(continued)

Table 5.11 (continued)

Structural relation			R.W.	S.E.	C.R.	S.R.W	SMC
TRANSPY3	←	cTRANSPY	1.253	0.079	15.779	0.774	0.6
TRANSPY4	←	cTRANSPY	1.034	0.071	14.662	0.735	0.54
TRU_COF1	←	cTRU_COF	1.22	0.073	16.619	0.792	0.627
TRU_COF2	←	cTRU_COF	1.263	0.071	17.901	0.832	0.692
TRU_COF3	←	cTRU_COF	1.452	0.071	20.557	0.905	0.819
TRU_COF4	←	cTRU_COF	1.418	0.07	20.24	0.897	0.805
TRU_COF5	←	cTRU_COF	1.436	0.073	19.748	0.884	0.781

Legend R.W Regression weight, *S.E* Standard error, *C.R* Critical ratio, *S.R.W* Standardized regression Weights, *S.M.C* Squared multiple correlation

5.10.3 Construct Validity Assessment

Construct validity refers to the ability of indicators or measures of a construct to measure what they are designed for (Brown 1996; Hair et al. 2010). Convergent validity is used in this research to measure construct validity (Hair et al. 2010). Convergent validity refers to reaching same results from performing a number of different methods on the same construct (Hair et al. 2010; Venkatraman and Grant 1986). Convergent validity can be examined using standardized loadings, Average Variance Extracted (AVE) and Composite Reliability (CR). Acceptable value for standardized loading has been discussed in Sect. 5.10.2, whereas the acceptable values for AVE and CR are shown in Table 5.12.

The CR and AVE values are computed using formulae suggested in the literature (Fornell and Larcker 1981; Hair et al. 2010). However, this research uses ready tools for calculating these values to avoid any human error. To confirm correctness, a number of different tools and calculators were used, which computed the same CR and AVE values (Table 5.13). The CR and AVE values are higher than 0.7 and 0.5, respectively, suggesting a good validity assessment of the measurement model.

5.11 Path Analysis

Path analysis is conducted for testing the proposed hypotheses in the conceptual model. As pointed out in the previous chapters, the conceptual model for this research consists of nine variables and eight hypotheses. Table 5.14 and Fig. 5.2 present results of path analysis conducted using AMOS.

Table 5.14 shows the path analysis results, where all eight hypotheses proposed for this research are supported. E-government has a significant negative effect on transformation ($b = -0.140$, $t = -11.6$, ***), thus providing support for H1a. Technology also shows a significant negative effect on transformation ($b = -0.694$, $t = -57.8$, ***) which support H1b. Expectations show a significant positive effect

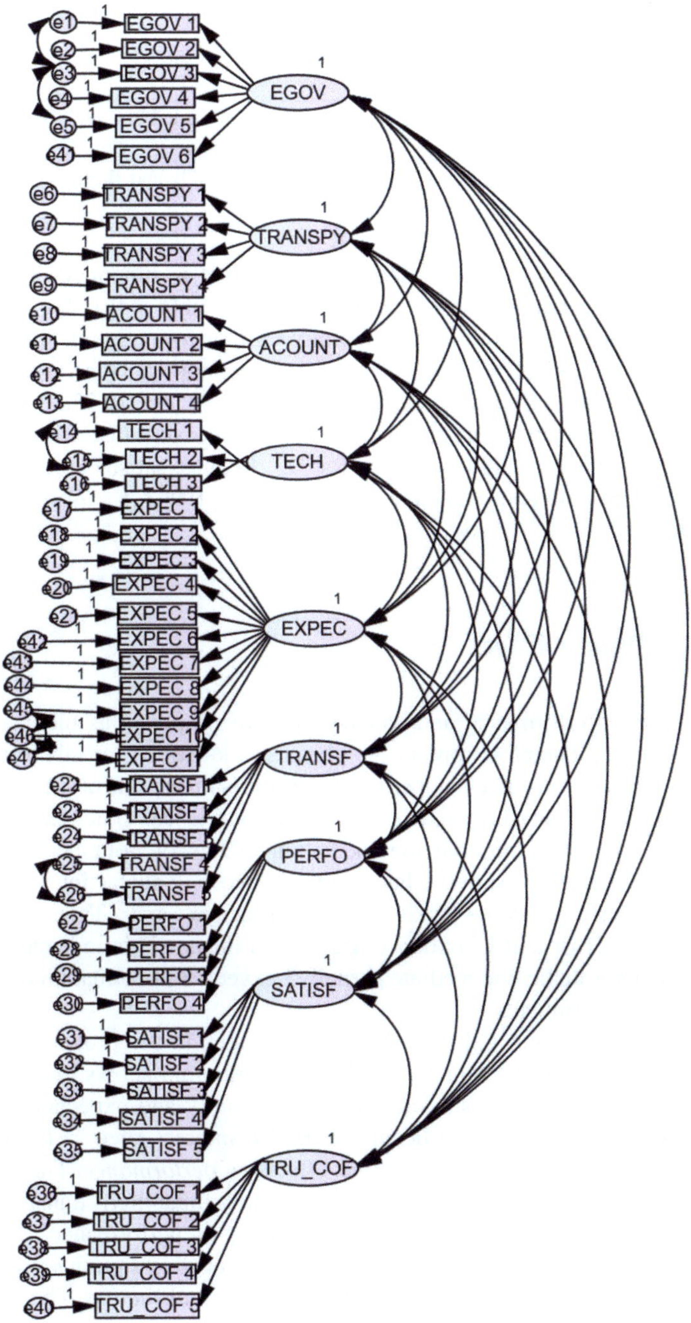

Fig. 5.1 Measurement model

Table 5.12 Recommended values for AVE and CR

Parameters	Recommended value	References
Average Variance Extracted (AVE)	>=0.5	Fornell and Larcker (1981), Hair et al. (2010)
Composite Reliability (CR)	>=0.7	Nunnally and Bernstein (1994)

on transformation (b = 0.323, t = 26.9, ***), so H1c is supported. Transparency also shows a significant positive effect on transformation (b = 0.154, t = 12.8, ***), so H1d is supported. Impact of accountability on transformation is also significant and positive (b = 0.605, t = 50.4, ***), so H1e is supported. Transformation shows a positive significant effect on performance (b = 0.957, t = 79.75, ***), so H2 is supported. Performance has a significant positive effect on satisfaction (b = 0.996, t = 19.92, ***), thus providing support for H3. Finally, satisfaction also shows a significant positive effect on trust and confidence (b = 0.963, t = 74.07, ***) which support H4.

5.12 Mediation Effect

Two constructs, performance and satisfaction, are proposed as mediators in the conceptual model. Therefore, one of the objectives identified for this research is to examine the mediation effect of performance and satisfaction on the relationship between transformation and citizens' trust and confidence. Outcomes of the path analysis are utilized to observe the mediation effects of both performance and satisfaction. Table 5.15 shows that paths between Satisfaction → Trust and Confidence, Performance → Trust and Confidence and Transformation of Government → Trust and Confidence are all significant. This indicates that both, performance and satisfaction mediate partially between transformation and trust and confidence in government.

In addition, direct and indirect effects of all paths in the proposed conceptual model are presented in the four figures below. Figure 5.3 shows that all paths for e-government, technology, transparency, accountability and expectation on *transformation* are having direct significant effects. No indirect effect is found here.

Figure 5.4 shows the direct and indirect effects on *performance*. The direct effect is between transformation and performance. Accountability, transparency and expectation have indirect positive significant effects on performance. On the other hand, e-government and technology have indirect negative significant effects.

Figure 5.5 shows the direct and indirect effects on *satisfaction*. The direct effect is between performance and satisfaction. Accountability, transparency, expectation and transformation have indirect positive significant effects on satisfaction. E-government and technology have indirect negative significant effects.

Table 5.13 AVE and CR Values of the Measurement Model

	CR	AVE	cSATISF	cEGOV	cTRANSPY	cACOUNT	cTECH	cEXPEC	cTRANSF	cPERFO	cTRU_COF
cSATISF	0.932	0.733	0.856								
cEGOV	0.897	0.594	0.756	0.771							
cTRANSPY	0.844	0.576	0.754	0.83	0.759						
cACOUNT	0.862	0.61	0.738	0.796	0.899	0.781					
cTECH	0.771	0.53	0.782	0.769	0.887	0.966	0.728				
cEXPEC	0.946	0.614	0.81	0.731	0.846	0.882	0.896	0.783			
cTRANSF	0.925	0.711	0.608	0.569	0.773	0.791	0.74	0.855	0.843		
cPERFO	0.899	0.691	0.948	0.783	0.791	0.775	0.796	0.821	0.656	0.831	
cTRU_COF	0.936	0.745	0.791	0.674	0.75	0.785	0.771	0.85	0.785	0.774	0.863

Table 5.14 Path analysis results

Hypotheses #	Path	Standardized coefficient (t)P	Results
H1c	EXPEC → TRANSF	0.323(26.9166667)***	Supported
H1b	TECH → TRANSF	−0.694(−57.8333333)***	Supported
H1a	EGOV → TRANSF	−0.140(−11.6666667)***	Supported
H1d	TRANSPY → TRANSF	0.154(12.8333333)***	Supported
H1e	ACOUNT → TRANSF	0.605(50.4166667)***	Supported
H2	TRANSF → PERFO	0.957(79.75)***	Supported
H3	PERFO → SATISF	0.996(19.92)***	Supported
H4	SATISF → TRU_COF	0.963(74.0769231)***	Supported

Note $*p < 0.05$, $**p < 0.01$, $***p < 0.001$

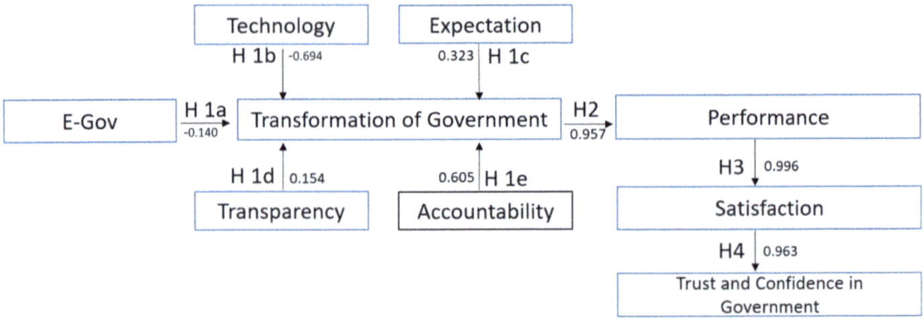

Fig. 5.2 Path analysis results

Table 5.15 Standardized regression weights

Path	Estimate	P
EXPEC → TRANSF	0.323	***
TECH → TRANSF	−0.694	***
EGOV → TRANSF	−0.140	***
TRANSPY → TRANSF	0.154	***
ACOUNT → TRANSF	0.605	***
TRANSF → PERFO	0.957	***
PERFO → SATISF	0.996	***
SATISF → TRU_COF	0.963	***
TRANSF → TRU_COF	0.918	***
PERFO → TRU_COF	0.959	***

Note $*p < 0.05$, $**p < 0.01$, $***p < 0.001$

Figure 5.6 shows the direct and indirect effects on *trust* and *confidence*. The direct effect is between satisfaction and trust and confidence. Accountability, transparency, expectation, transformation and performance have indirect positive significant effects on citizens' trust and confidence. E-government and technology, on the other hand, have indirect negative significant effects.

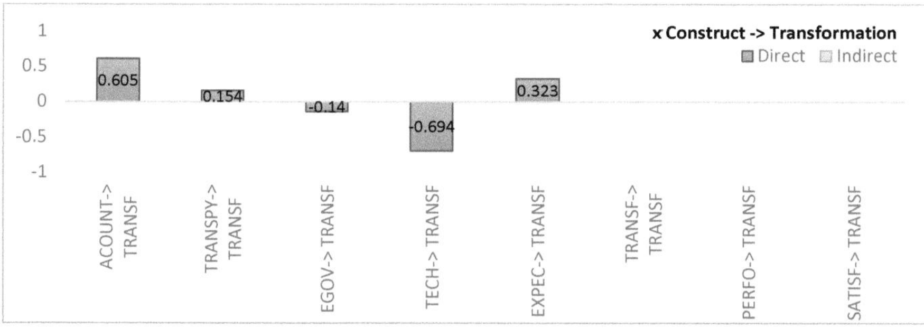

Fig. 5.3 Total effects of direct and indirect paths on transformation

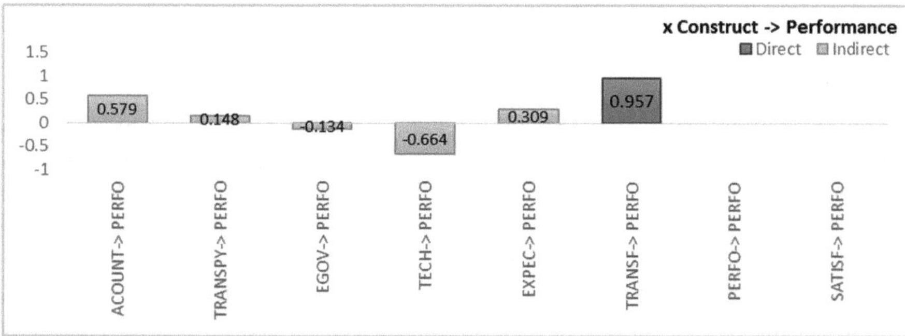

Fig. 5.4 Total effects of direct and indirect paths on performance

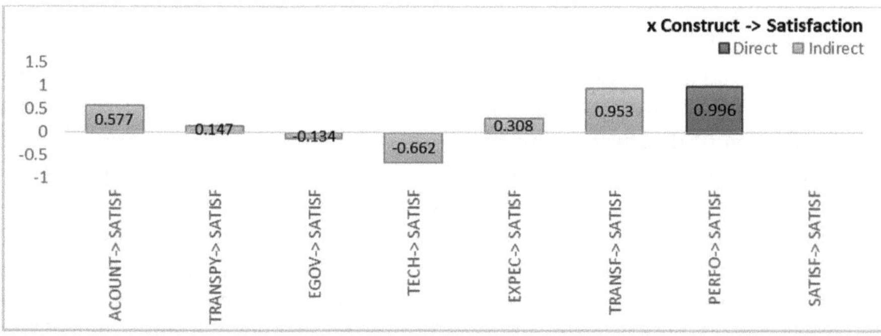

Fig. 5.5 Total effects of direct and indirect paths on satisfaction

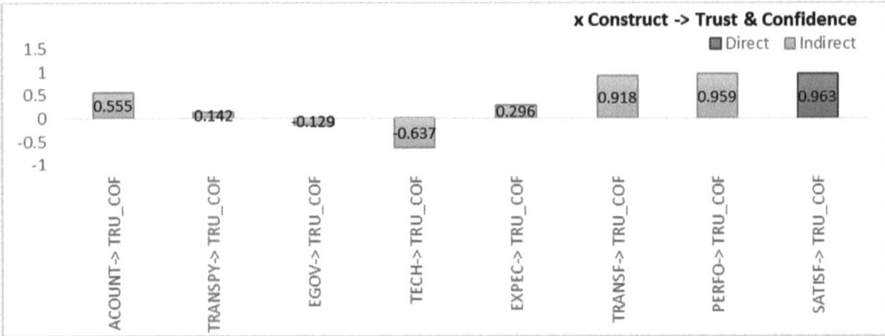

Fig. 5.6 Total effects of direct and indirect paths on trust and confidence

5.13 Summary

This chapter presents data analysis, including results from different tests, and findings from CFA and path analysis. It starts with illustrating response rate and sample size of the online survey, followed by a profile of the respondents. There was no gender or age bias in the respondent profile, and most respondents were highly educated and well paid.

In order to identify potential problems with variables, early in the process, as well as preparing the variables for a smooth SEM phase, EFA was employed. This was followed by reliability and validity testing of the research instrument to ensure consistency and accuracy of the research. Next, descriptive statistics were presented, with means and standard deviation for all items of the research instrument.

In order to describe the degree of relationship between different variables, a correlation matrix was employed to confirm that there was significant correlation amongst the variables. Another important test conducted was the Skewness and Kurtosis test for validating the normality of data distribution. This test proved that the distribution of data was normal.

SEM was chosen to validate the fitness of the conceptual model and test the hypotheses by performing CFA and path analysis. CFA resulted in a good fit for the measurement model. Values for standardized loadings, critical rations and R squares were in line with the recommended values. Furthermore, construct validity was examined by adopting convergent validity, which resulted in good validity of the measurement model. Path analysis confirmed that all the eight hypotheses suggested for this research were supported by the gathered data. Mediation effects were also analysed, which illustrate that both performance and satisfaction mediate partially between transformation and citizens' trust and confidence in government. Finally, the direct and indirect effects of all paths of the proposed conceptual model were presented and analysed. The Next chapter will discuss the findings of this research.

References

Bartko JJ (1966) The intraclass correlation coefficient as a measure of reliability. Psychol Rep 19 (1):3–11
Brown JD (1996) Testing in language programs. Prentice Hall Regents, Upper Saddle River
Cabrera-Nguyen P (2010) Author guidelines for reporting scale development and validation results. J Soc Soc Work Res 1(2):99–103
Comrey A, Lee H (1992) A first course in factor analysis. Lawrence Erlbaum Associates, Hillsdale
Field A (2006) Discovering statistics using SPSS, 2nd edn. Sage, London
Fornell C, Larcker DF (1981) Evaluating structural equation models with unobservable variables and measurement error. J Mark Res 18(1):39–50
Fowler FJ Jr (2002) Survey research methods. Sage Publications Inc., London
Hair JF, Tatham RL, Anderson RE, Black W (2006) Multivariate data analysis. Pearson Prentice Hall, Upper Saddle River
Hair JF, Anderson RE, Babin BJ, Black WC (2010) Multivariate data analysis: a global perspective, vol 7. Pearson, Upper Saddle River
Henson RK, Roberts JK (2006) Use of exploratory factor analysis in published research: common errors and some comment on improved practice. Educ Psychol Measur 66(3):393–416
Hooper D, Coughlan J, Mullen M (2008) Structural equation modelling: guidelines for determining model fit. Articles p 2
Hox JJ, Bechger TM (1998) An introduction to structural equation modelling. Fam Sci Rev 11:354–373
Hu L-T, Bentler PM (1999) Cutoff criteria for fit indexes in covariance structure analysis: conventional criteria versus new alternatives. Struct Equ Model 6:1–55
Iacobucci D (2010) Structural equations modeling: fit indices, sample size, and advanced topics
Jackson DL, Gillaspy JA Jr, Purc-Stephenson R (2009) Reporting practices in confirmatory factor analysis: an overview and some recommendations. Psychol Methods 14(1):6
Lee Rodgers J, Nicewander WA (1988) Thirteen ways to look at the correlation coefficient. Am Stat 42(1):59–66
Lee J, Lee JN, Tan BC (2015) Antecedents of cognitive trust and affective distrust and their mediating roles in building customer loyalty. Inf Syst Front 17(1):159–175
Li DX (1999) Value at risk based on the volatility. Skewness and kurtosis. RiskMetrics Group
Nunnally JC, Bernstein IH (1994) Psychometric theory, 3rd edn. McGraw-Hill, New York
Pallant J (2010) SPSS survival manual, 4th edn. Allen and Unwin Book Publishers, Australia
Pigott TD (2001) A review of methods for missing data. Educ Res Eval 7(4):353–383
Robinson JP, Shaver PR, Wrightsman LS (1991) Criteria for scale selection and evaluation. Measures Pers Soc Psychol Attitudes 1(3):1–16
Schreiber JB, Nora A, Stage FK, Barlow EA, King J (2006) Reporting structural equation modelling and confirmatory factor analysis results: a review. J Educ Res 99(6):323–338
Sekaran U (2000) Research methods for business: a skill-building approach. Willey, USA
Suhr D (2006) The basics of structural equation modeling. In: SAS User Group of the Western Region of the United States (WUSS), Irvine
Tabachnick BG, Fidell LS, Osterlind SJ (2001) Using multivariate statistics. Pearson, New York
Taylor R (1990) Interpretation of the correlation coefficient: a basic review. J Diagn Med Sonography 6(1):35–39
Thompson B (2004) Exploratory and confirmatory factor analysis: understanding concepts and applications. American Psychological Association
Venkatraman N, Grant JH (1986) Construct measurement in organizational strategy research: a critique and proposal. Acad Manag Rev 11(1):71–87
Williams B, Onsman A, Brown T (2010) Exploratory factor analysis: a five-step guide for novices. Australas J Paramedicine 8(3)
Worthington R, Whittaker T (2006) Scale development research: a content analysis and recommendations for best practices. Counseling Psychol 34:806–838

Chapter 6
Discussion

6.1 Introduction

Chapter 5 presented outcomes of the data analysis conducted on the collected data from ordinary citizens living in Bahrain. The data analysis covered different tests performed and findings of the CFA and path analysis. The eight hypotheses suggested for this research were supported by the empirical findings.

This chapter discusses the findings of the data analysis presented in Chap. 5 as well as mapping the findings to the gaps identified and the three questions agreed for this research. The outcomes of the empirical findings of this research are consistent with the literature review. In this chapter, answers to the three research questions and results of the eight hypotheses are thoroughly discussed, justified, explained and linked to the practical side. Moreover, the findings of this research illustrate that transformation of government has a significant positive effect on citizens' trust and confidence. It is interesting to find that e-government and technology are not sufficient for achieving a true transformed government. Three other factors should be considered, which are citizens' expectations, adoption of transparency and activating accountability.

This chapter is structured as follows. Section 6.2 provides an overview of the research in hand while in Sect. 6.3 the concept of citizens' trust and confidence in government and transformation of government is revisited. In Sect. 6.4, instrument validation process and results are presented. This is followed by Sect. 6.5, which includes an overview of the findings, answering the three research questions, presenting and discussing outcomes of the hypotheses testing, clarifying the role of the mediators and finally presenting the direct and indirect effects of all paths of the proposed conceptual model. Some thoughts on the empirical findings are presented in Sect. 6.6. The last Sect. 6.7, summarizes the overall chapter.

M. Mahmood, *Does Digital Transformation of Government Lead to Enhanced Citizens' Trust and Confidence in Government?*, Springer Theses,
https://doi.org/10.1007/978-3-030-01759-0_6

6.2 Overview of the Research

The aim of this research was to investigate the influence of transformation of government on citizens' trust and confidence in government from citizens' perspective. Transformation of Government was defined as the fundamental changes to the way core functions of government are performed to achieve noticeable gains in performance and efficiency In doing so, three research questions were posited for this research, which were: (1) what factors influence transformation of government, (2) how these factors influence transformation, and (3) how transformation of government can be related to trust and confidence in citizens. In order to fulfil the aim and answer the three research questions, literature review was performed using secondary and primary sources. During this phase, key factors influencing transformation of government and trust and confidence in government were identified and explained. A conceptual model was then developed using the model developed by Morgeson et al. (2011) as a base model and taking into account the factors identified during the literature phase. The defined constructs and relationships within the conceptual model were supported by appropriate theories. In terms of research methodology, this research adopted a quantitative methodology using an online survey, targeting randomly, ordinary citizens of the Kingdom of Bahrain. In order to validate the conceptual model and ensure reliability of the data, a pilot survey was conducted prior to conducting the major survey. SEM was employed for this research as multivariate analysis technique. CFA and path analysis were performed which resulted in a good fit of the proposed conceptual model and supporting all hypotheses set for this research. Findings of the data analysis are discussed in details in the below sections of this chapter.

6.3 Revisiting the Concept of Citizen's Trust and Confidence in Government and Transformation of Government

The literature review presented in the previous chapters showed that citizens' trust in their government has been declining during the last two decades (Bean 2015; Edwards 2015; Morgeson et al. 2011; Teo et al. 2008; World Employment and Social Outlook Trend 2015, 2016, 2017). E-government was seen as a way of reducing this decline when introduced and implemented in different parts of the world (Morgeson et al. 2011; Teo et al. 2008; Tolbert and Mossberger 2006). During the last two decades, a large sum of money has been spent on various e-government projects around the world as illustrated in the Table 6.1.

However, the introduction of e-government has failed to meet the desired outcomes nor helped in reversing the decline in citizens' trust and confidence in government due to conflicting conclusions on the relation between e-government and citizens' trust in government (Bannister and Connolly 2011; Kim et al. 2009;

Table 6.1 Money spent on e-government projects

Country	Amount	Reference
USA—as of 2014	$36,65 billons since 1992	Mukhoryanova et al. (2016)
South Korea—as of 2014	$1.6 billons since 2003	Mukhoryanova et al. (2016)
Russia—as of 2014	$0,18 billons since 2002	Mukhoryanova et al. (2016)
UK—2001	$520 millions	Basu (2004)
India—2001	$189 millions	Basu (2004)
1129 investment lending projects in 135 countries funded by the World Bank	$292, 677 millions since 1995	World Bank (2017)

Table 6.2 Failing e-government projects

Project	Amount lost	Reference
C-Nomis (UK)	£2 billion	The Economist (Feb, 2008)
e-Boarder system (UK)	£224 millions	The Guardian (19 August, 2014)
BBC—Video Archives System (UK)	£100 millions	The Guardian (19 August, 2014)
Ministry of Justice—Back Office Project (UK)	£56 millions	The Guardian (19 August, 2014)
NHS's National Programme for IT (UK)	£10 billions	The Guardian (19 August, 2014)
Common Agricultural Policy Delivery Programme	£642 millions since 2005	House of Commons (Feb, 2017)
Healthcase.gov (USA)	$ 630 millions	Anthopoulos et al. (2016)

Morgeson et al. 2011; Weerakkody et al. 2009; Welch et al. 2005). In the UK, many of the large scale transformation projects that were implemented under the e-government agenda failed to meet their outcomes as illustrated in Table 6.2.

Some scholars have posited that transformation of government has the potential to reverse the decline in citizens' trust and confidence in government (Bannister and Connolly 2011; Waller and Weerakkody 2016; Zwahr et al. 2005). In addition to transformation of government, other factors identified in the literature that influence citizens' trust and confidence in government include e-government (Morgeson et al. 2011; Tolbert and Mossberger 2006), technology (Morgeson et al. 2011; Tolbert and Mossberger 2006), transparency (Bannister and Connolly 2011; Kim et al. 2009), accountability (Bannister and Connolly 2011; Kim et al. 2009), citizens' expectations (Morgeson and Petrescu 2011; Morgeson et al. 2011), transformation of government (Bannister and Connolly 2011; Waller and Weerakkody 2016; Zwahr et al. 2005), government performance (Bouckaert et al. 2005; Morgeson et al. 2011; Van de Walle and Bouckaert 2003; Van de Walle et al. 2008) and citizens' satisfactions (Bouckaert et al. 2005; Morgeson et al. 2011; Teo et al. 2008; Van de Walle and Bouckaert 2003; Van de Walle et al. 2008).

Despite e-government initiatives starting late in GCC countries compared to other parts of the world such as Europe and North America, they have reached advanced stages and achieved high rankings in several GCC countries as per the United Nations E-Government Survey Reports released in 2012, 2014 and 2016. These advanced levels could have not been achieved without the investments made in the region on e-government initiatives. Yet, the United Nations E-Government Survey Report 2016 highlighted that e-participation still remains an issue in both the developed and developing countries. Limited studies that have focused on the GCC region have confirmed that citzens' trust and confidence plays a role in this issue (Al-Shafi and Weerakkody 2008; AlSobhi et al. 2010). Compared to the rest of the world, there is lack of studies conducted in GCC countries, which investigated the influence that transformation of government has on citizens' trust and confidence in government. These reasons make the GCC region an attractive region to investigate the influence of transformation of government on citizens' trust and confidence in government. In order to investigate the influence of transformation of government on the citizens' trust and confidence in government, a conceptual model was developed building upon the model proposed by Morgeson et al. (2011) and supported by several other theories. Five factors which are critical for the context of transformation of government, which are currently discussed separately in the literature are reviewed and synthesized to propose hypotheses to examine their relationships with transformation of government. The conceptual model was validated in Bahrain and proven functioning well as all eight hypotheses proposed for this research were supported based on 313 responses received from citizens' living in Bahrain.

It is worth pointing out that previous theoretical models and frameworks focused on the relationship between trust in government and take-up of e-government systems (Abu-Shanab and Al-Azzam 2012; Bélanger and Carter 2008; Carter and Bélanger 2005; Colesca 2009; Navarrete 2010; Teo et al. 2008) and the effect of e-government on trust in governments (Grimmelikhuijsen 2009; McNeal et al. 2008; Morgeson et al. 2011; Pina et al. 2009; Pina and Royo 2009; Tolbert and Mossberger 2006). Welch et al. (2005) on the other hand covered some elements of transformation of government and trust of government with an emphasis on e-government systems rather than digital 'transformation of government' (i.e. that was focused on changes to the way core functions of government are performed through ICT).

6.4 Instrument Validation

In order to validate the findings of the research, it is essential to conduct the reliability and validity of the research instrument before and after the data collection (Hair et al. 2010; Straub el al., 2004). Cronbach's alpha was used to measure the reliability. Alpha values at 0.7 were considered as acceptable, exceeding 0.7 were good, while those below 0.7 were considered as poor (Sekaran 2000). On the other hand, internal consistency measure was adopted for measuring validity; specifically inter-item correlation and item to total correlation of items under each construct were measured. Minimum correlation value was set as acceptable at 0.3 and the maximum was set at 0.8 for the inter-item correlation measure, whereas minimum correlation value was set as acceptable at 0.5 for item to total correlation measure (Robinson et al. 1991a). Results of the reliability and validity analysis conducted on the pilot and main surveys' instruments showed that values of Cronbach's alpha, Inter-item correlation and Item-to total correlation were exceeding 0.7, 0.3 and 0.5 respectively. Therefore, it can be concluded that the research instruments used for the pilot and main surveys were valid and reliable.

Following adopting SEM for this research and performing CFA, convergent validity was used to measure construct validity (Hair et al. 2010). Convergent validity was examined through using standardized loadings of all items, AVE and CR. Acceptable value for the Standardized loadings were achieved as shown under Sect. 5.10.2. The CR and AVE of all the constructs as illustrated in Table 5.13 were higher than 0.7 and 0.5 respectively. As such, convergent validity resulted in a good validity of the measurement model.

6.5 Significance of the Empirical Findings

6.5.1 Overview of the Findings

Following the literature review and to fulfil the aim and objectives agreed for this research, the developed conceptual model consisted of nine constructs and eight hypotheses amongst these constructs, which were explained, in details in Chap. 3. The conceptual model was validated and accordingly path analysis was conducted and the results are illustrated in Table 6.3. It should be noted that all answers represent citizens' perception of every defined construct and relationship within the conceptual model.

Results of the path analysis show that the eight hypotheses suggested for this research are supported. In details, e-government has a significant negative effect on transformation ($b = -0.140$, $-t = 11.6$, ***), thus providing support for H1a.

Table 6.3 Path analysis results

Hypotheses #	Path	Standardized coefficient $(t)P$	Results
H1c	EXPEC → TRANSF	0.323(26.9166667)***	Supported
H1b	TECH → TRANSF	−0.694(−57.8333333)***	Supported
H1a	EGOV → TRANSF	−0.140(−11.6666667)***	Supported
H1d	TRANSPY → TRANSF	0.154(12.8333333)***	Supported
H1e	ACOUNT → TRANSF	0.605(50.4166667)***	Supported
H2	TRANSF → PERFO	0.957(79.75)***	Supported
H3	PERFO → SATISF	0.996(19.92)***	Supported
H4	SATISF → TRU_COF	0.963(74.0769231)***	Supported

Note *$p < 0.05$, **$p < 0.01$, ***$p < 0.001$

Technology also shows a significant negative effect on transformation ($b = -0.694$, $t = -57.8$, ***) which support H1b. Expectations shows a significant positive effect on transformation ($b = 0.323$, $t = 26.9$, ***), so H1c is supported. Transparency also shows a significant positive effect on transformation ($b = 0.154$, $t = 12.8$, ***), so H1d is supported. Impact of accountability on transformation is also significant positive ($b = 0.605$, $t = 50.4$, ***), so H1e is supported. Transformation shows a positive significant effect on performance ($b = 0.957$, $t = 79.75$, ***), so H2 is supported. Performance as well has a significant positive effect on satisfaction $b = 0.996$, $t = 19.92$, ***), thus providing support for H3. Finally, satisfaction also shows a significant positive effect on trust and confidence ($b = 0.963$, $t = 74.07$, ***) which support H4.

6.5.2 Answers to the Research Questions

Three questions were set for this research, which were: (1) what factors influence transformation of government, (2) how these factors influence transformation of government, and (3) how transformation of government can be related to trust and confidence in citizens. Based on the results presented in the previous section, all eight hypotheses suggested for this research were supported. Therefore, the below paragraphs provide answers to the three research questions.

6.5.2.1 Research Question Q1

The literature review identified eight factors influencing citizens' trust and confidence in government being e-government (Morgeson et al. 2011; Tolbert and Mossberger 2006), technology (Morgeson et al. 2011; Tolbert and Mossberger 2006), transparency (Bannister and Connolly 2011; Kim et al. 2009), accountability (Bannister and Connolly 2011; Kim et al. 2009), citizens' expectations (Morgeson and Petrescu 2011; Morgeson et al. 2011), transformation of government (Bannister and Connolly 2011; Waller and Weerakkody 2016; Zwahr et al. 2005), government performance (Bouckaert et al. 2005; Morgeson et al. 2011; Van de Walle and Bouckaert 2003; Van de Walle et al. 2008) and citizens' satisfactions (Bouckaert et al. 2005; Morgeson et al. 2011; Teo et al. 2008; Van de Walle and Bouckaert 2003; Van de Walle et al. 2008).

The conceptual model developed for this research investigates the relationship between transformation of government and citizens' trust and confidence in government. For this purpose, five factors supported by the literature were hypothesized to influence transformation of government which were e-government (Bannister and Connolly 2011; Bellamy and Taylor 1998), technology (Bannister and Connolly 2011; Bingham 2010; Bonham et al. 2001; Kim et al. 2009; Weerakkody et al. 2009), expectation (Dalton 2005; Graham and Avery 2013; Welch et al. 2005), transparency (Bannister and Connolly 2011; Brown 1999;

Fountain 2001; Northrup and Thorson 2003) and accountability (Bannister and Connolly 2011; Bingham 2010; Kim et al. 2009; Norquist 2007). Findings of the research support the relationships between the five factors mentioned above and transformation of government and further, all five factors have significant effect on transformation of government as can be seen in Table 6.3.

The above means citizens perceive that in order to have a real, impactful and successful transformed government five factors should be considered which are (1) the introduction of e-government as an officially promoted system in the country, (2) adoption of latest technologies by all government agencies that support digital initiatives and shifting the way government functions, (3) meet citizens' expectation from the government and its services (4) adoption of transparency in its functions and operations and (5) finally practicing accountability where the government or the concerned government agency is fully accountable to its citizens through being ready to provide justification for its conduct. This answers research question Q1 identified for this research.

6.5.2.2 Research Question Q2

As stated above, five factors are identified which are influencing transformation of government. Out of these, three factors have positive effect on transformation of government, which are citizens' expectations, transparency and accountability. The literature confirms the relationships between the three factors and transformation of government as shown in the above section. The positive effects of transparency and accountability on transformation of government are logical in practice as the general agenda of transformation comes by default with accountability and transparency (Bannister and Connolly 2011). Indeed, managing and meeting citizens' expectations and demands in terms of expected services, ease of performing processes and procedures, timeline for processes and required evidence have a positive effect on transformation of government.

On the other hand, e-government and technology have negative effect on transformation of government. The literature related to these relationships show that there are conflicting views on the role of e-government and technology in the context of transforming government. Reflecting on such conflicting views, some researchers have argued that e-government and technology can help in transforming government (Al-Shafi and Weerakkody 2008, 2010; Srivastava and Teo 2009; Tolbert and Mossberger 2006; Welch et al. 2005; West 2004). Other researchers have pointed out that many e-government projects failed (Alsaeed et al. 2014; Anthopoulos et al. 2016; Bannister and Connolly 2011; Choi et al. 2016; Das Aundhe et al. 2016; Gunawong and Gao 2017; Omar et al. 2017; Sehli et al. 2016; Waller and Weerakkody 2016). In practice, the reasons for the negative effect of e-government and technology on transformation of government may be linked to the specific context and conditions of Bahrain (i.e. demographic and/or socio-cultural issues and relative newness of e-government), which is where the study conducted. This is further explained under the hypotheses related to e-government and transformation of government as well as technology and transformation of government. This answers research question Q2 identified for this research.

6.5.2.3 Research Question Q3

As per the literature, there is a lack of knowledge on how transformation of government influences citizens' trust and confidence in government. In fact, this is the key gap found in this study and thus the research in hand attempts to address it and in doing so, research question Q3 was posited.

Following the above answers to research Q1 and Q2, the answer to research Q3 is relatively clear. As per the findings of this research, transformation of government has a positive significant effect on citizens' trust and confidence mediated by performance of government and citizens' satisfaction. This relation is illustrated in Table 6.3 above and explained in details under Sects. 5.11 and 5.12. In practice, this means that citizens' trust and confidence in government will be enhanced if there is a real transformation of government, which can be achieved through considering and adopting five factors to be part of the transformation agenda. The five factors as presented above are (1) the introduction of e-government as an officially promoted system in the country, (2) adoption of latest technologies by all government agencies that support digital initiatives and shifting the way government function and work, (3) meet and manage citizens' expectations and (4) and (5) adoption of transparency in all functions, activities and operations of the government as well as the government being fully accountable to its citizens. This answers research question Q3 as well as bridging the gap identified in this research.

The knowledge gained through answering the three research questions may enhance citizens' trust and confidence in government as well helping in reversing its decline.

6.5.3 Results of the Hypotheses Testing

As mentioned previously, the research in hand proposed eight hypotheses amongst the nine constructs defined within the conceptual model. All eight hypotheses were supported by the empirical findings of this research, which represent citizens' perception of every defined construct and relationship within the conceptual model. The sections that follow discuss each hypothesis separately and confirm whether each hypothesis is confirmed by the collected data or not.

6.5.3.1 H1a E-Government and Transformation of Government

As per the literature, e-government was viewed as a solution to reverse the decline in citizens' and confidence in government as well as helping to transform the way government functions and delivers services (Al-Shafi and Weerakkody 2008, 2010; Srivastava and Teo 2009; Tolbert and Mossberger 2006; Welch et al. 2005; West 2004). Additionally, e-government was viewed as a means to enable transparency and promote accountability (Roztocki and Weistroffer 2016). The literature also suggests that many e-government based initiatives failed (Anthopoulos et al. 2016; Alsaeed et al. 2014; Bannister and Connolly 2011; Choi et al. 2016; Das Aundhe et al. 2016; Gunawong and Gao 2017; Omar et al. 2017; Sehli et al. 2016; Waller and Weerakkody 2016) and thus citizens' trust and confidence has continued to decline (Bannister and Connolly 2011; Bean 2015; Edwards 2015; Morgeson et al. 2011; Teo et al. 2008; West 2004; World Employment and Social Outlook Trends 2015, 2016, 2017). To support this view, Table 6.1 lists amounts spent on e-government projects, particularly in the UK. Despite these large investments, Table 6.2 lists a number of failing e-government projects. The focus of many of these e-government projects was technical which means provisioning of portals, websites and other digital means for using e-government services (Omar et al. 2017; Waller and Weerakkody 2016). As such, many e-government initiatives did not achieve the desired outcomes nor resulted in transformed governments (in a way that would result in real changes to the way government functions of delivers services) (Bannister and Connolly 2011; Waller and Weerakkody 2016; Zwahr et al. 2005).

Result of H1a testing shows that e-government has a significant negative effect on transformation ($b = -0.140$, $t = -11.6$, ***), thus providing support for H1a. This finding is in line with outcomes of prior researches (Anthopoulos et al. 2016; Alsaeed et al. 2014; Bannister and Connolly 2011; Choi et al. 2016; Das Aundhe et al. 2016; Gunawong and Gao 2017; Omar et al. 2017; Sehli et al. 2016; Waller and Weerakkody 2016). Despite the fact that Bahrain has an advanced e-government platform, the United Nations e-Government Surveys released in 2014 and 2016 confirm the finding of H1a from two perspectives. First, Bahrain was ranked 24th globally in the 2016 EGDI index whereas it ranked 18 globally in the 2014 report. Second, Bahrain was ranked 32nd globally in the e-participation sub-index of the 2016 UN report whereas it ranked 14th globally as per the 2014 UN report.

Despite the fact that respondents to the survey use internet, the reasons for the negative effect of e-government on transformation of government may be linked to the specific context of the place where this study was conducted—Bahrain. For instance, skills needed to use e-government services, trust in e-government systems, security and privacy concerns, not interested in services provide by e-government, awareness issues, continued use of personal contacts within government agencies to fulfil needs instead of using e-government systems, poor experience of using e-government systems, and finally lack of training and education provided to citizens to use e-government systems may all influence citizens perception towards e-government. Apart from these reasons, the negative effect may be related to the technical oriented focus of e-government systems in Bahrain. Moving forward, these potential reasons should be taken into account by the government and concerned agencies in Bahrain so that successful transformation of government can be achieved.

The key message here is that e-government cannot work alone and thus other factors should be considered in parallel for meeting the desired results.

6.5.3.2 H1b Technology and Transformation of Government

Technology is closely related with e-government and as such, the majority of arguments and recommendations presented in the previous section are applicable here too. Technology is more of a wider term that refers to the use of information technology in all government agencies to perform and function their businesses and duties (Al Rub, 2006). This includes integration with the e-government system as well as provisioning of the government agency's specific services. The literature pointed out that technology plays a key role in enabling transformation of government and enhancing government performance (Bannister and Connolly 2011; Kim et al. 2009). Furthermore, transparency and accountability are enhanced as a result of using technology (Bannister and Connolly 2011; Kim et al. 2009; Norquist 2007).

As stated in the previous section, technology in general and e-government in particular were proposed as an integrated solution to reverse the decline in citizens' trust and confidence in government as well as transform the government. Since technology is working closely with e-government, the same conflicting views presented under e-government are applicable here. Some say it helps in achieving the desired form of transformed government (Al-Shafi and Weerakkody 2008, 2010; Srivastava and Teo 2009; Tolbert and Mossberger 2006; Welch et al. 2005; West 2004) whereas others say many e-government and technology based initiatives failed and did not achieve the expected results (Anthopoulos et al. 2016; Alsaeed et al. 2014; Bannister and Connolly 2011; Choi et al. 2016; Das Aundhe et al. 2016; Gunawong and Gao 2017; Omar et al. 2017; Sehli et al. 2016; Waller and Weerakkody 2016). Tables 6.1 and 6.2 support this view. For this reason, citizens' trust and confidence in government is still considered as an alarming issue that should be resolved (Bannister and Connolly 2011; Bean 2015; Edwards 2015; Morgeson et al. 2011; Teo et al. 2008; West 2004; World Employment and Social Outlook Trends 2015, 2016, 2017).

Result of H1b testing shows that technology has a significant negative effect on transformation ($b = -0.694$, $t = -57.8$, ***) which support H1b. This finding is in line with outcomes of prior research (Anthopoulos et al. 2016; Alsaeed et al. 2014; Bannister and Connolly 2011; Choi et al. 2016; Das Aundhe et al. 2016; Gunawong and Gao 2017; Omar et al. 2017; Sehli et al. 2016; Waller and Weerakkody 2016). Furthermore, United Nations e-Government Surveys released in 2014 and 2016 confirm the finding of H1b where Bahrain's ranking in the EGDI index and e-participation sub-index decreased by 6 and 18 levels respectively.

Many of the reasons highlighted above can be used here to explain the negative effect of technology on transformation of government such as skills needed, trust in the medium, security, privacy, training and awareness. Additionally, integration amongst government agencies as well as compatibility between systems in different government agencies to support the specifications of the e-government systems and standards may explain the negative effect.

The above potential reasons should be taken into account by the government and concerned agencies in Bahrain in moving forward with any transformation efforts in government. The key message here is that technology alone does not deliver transformed government nor result in enhancing trust in government (Bannister and Connolly 2011).

6.5.3.3 H1c Citizens' Expectation and Transformation of Government

Meeting citizens' expectation is considered as a key factor for achieving successful transformation of government and restoring citizens' trust in government (Nam 2012). The literature explained that citizens' expectation can be met through a number of mechanism including empowering, involving, engaging and consulting with citizens prior to and/or post launching of e-government services (Hanna 2009).

Result of H1c shows that expectation has a significant positive effect on transformation of government ($b = 0.323$, $t = 26.9$, ***), so H1c is supported. This finding is consistent with outcomes of the literature review (e.g. Hanna 2009; Nam 2012).

To interpret the finding of H1c, citizens perceive that their expectations are met and taken into consideration and thus successful transformation of government is achieved. In practice, it is believed that citizens' expectations are related to provisioning of services at the time promised by the government, offering prompt services, readiness of the government to respond to citizens' queries, government officials give attention to all, understand citizens' needs and have the knowledge to answer citizens' questions, citizens feel safe and confident when they perform their transactions, government informs citizens in advance of any changes to the services and government maintaining error-free-records.

The above are some parameters of citizens' expectations that should be taken into account by the government and concerned agencies in Bahrain in their e-government agenda and efforts to transform government.

6.5.3.4 H1d Transparency and Transformation of Government

One key element of the transformation agenda is transparency and it comes by default with accountability (Bannister and Connolly 2011). Moreover, it enhances performance of the government as well as citizens' trust in government (Bannister and Connolly 2011; Welch et al. 2005). The literature confirms that technology enhances further the implementation of transparency (Bannister and Connolly 2011; Kim et al. 2009; Welch et al. 2005). However, national culture may affect implementation of transparency in different countries (De Fine Licht 2011; Grimmelikhuijsen 2012; Grimmelikhuijsen et al. 2013; Hood 2006; O'Neill 2002; Roberts 2006; Tolbert and Mossberger 2006). The literature highlighted that transparency can be implemented in different forms; for instance the visibility of all government related information, processes and procedures to outsiders (Chen et al. 2003; Song and Lee 2013; Welch et al. 2005).

Result of H1d shows that transparency has a significant positive effect on transformation of government ($b = 0.154$, $t = 12.8$, ***), so H1d is supported. This finding is consistent with outcomes of the literature review (Bannister and Connolly 2011; Welch et al. 2005).

To interpret the finding of H1d, citizens perceive that when transparency is present, it results in successful transformation of government and enhances performance of government. In practice, transparency can be fulfilled through dissemination of government related information, processes, procedures, services, tracking applications, activities, transactions, policies, decisions, regulations and legal instruments as well as commissioning consulting process with the stakeholders. These findings offer valuable insights to the government in Bahrain and others elsewhere.

6.5.3.5 H1e Accountability and Transformation of Government

Both transparency and accountability come with the transformation agenda (Bannister and Connolly 2011) and result in improving the performance of the government and citizens' trust in government (Bannister and Connolly 2011; Kim et al. 2009; Norquist 2007). The literature highlighted that accountability means the government is ready to provide justification for its conduct to its citizens (Gray et al. 1987; Giddens 1984; Huse 2005; ISEA 1999; Swift 2001; Williams 1987).

Result of H1e shows that accountability has a significant positive effect on transformation of government ($b = 0.605$, $t = 50.4$, ***), so H1e is supported. This finding is consistent with outcomes of the literature review (Bannister and Connolly 2011; Kim et al. 2009; Norquist 2007).

To interpret the finding of H1d, citizens perceive that when accountability is practiced it results in successful transformation of government and enhances performance of government. In practice, accountability can be found where government provide justifications for its conduct, existence of appeal and escalations processes and budgets are used properly and in an authorized manner.

6.5.3.6 H2 Transformation of Government and Performance of Government

Successful transformation of government moves government from traditional to an innovative, digital, transparent and accountable government that meets citizens' expectations and demands. Indeed, it improves the performance of the government and enables it to be more effective and efficient (Hameed and Al-Shawabkha 2013; Seifert and Chung 2009; Waller and Weerakkody 2016; Zwahr et al. 2005).

Transformation here is closely associated with the word change (Bannister and Connolly 2011; Cabinet Office 2005; Moon and Norris 2005; Waller and Weerakkody 2016) meaning that it will significantly improve the processes and functioning of government compared to traditional or previous way of delivering services.

Result of H2 shows that transformation of government has a positive significant effect on performance ($b = 0.957$, $t = 79.75$, ***), so H2 is supported. This finding is consistent with outcomes of the literature review (Al-Shawabkha 2013; Bannister and Connolly 2011; Seifert and Chung 2009; Waller and Weerakkody 2016; Zwahr et al. 2005).

To interpret the finding of H2, citizens perceive that transformation of government that considers a number of key factors such as e-government, technology, citizens' expectations, transparency and accountability results in improving the performance of the government and changes the old government to an innovate and digital based one. In practice, it means the new government is ready to accept new ideas for implementing desired changes to be more efficient and effective, high-level officials in government are eager to do things differently, flexibility is adopted where procedures are changed quickly to meet new conditions and solve problems as they arise, transparency is adopted in all functions and activities of the government, the government is accountable for its conduct and they listen to citizens.

The above are some parameters of transformation of government that should be taken into consideration by the government and concerned agencies in Bahrain so that performance of the government is continually improved and enhanced.

6.5.3.7 H3 Performance of Government and Citizens' Satisfaction

The literature suggest that through being a transformed government, performance of government improves which leads to satisfied citizens with the government and its services (Morgeson et al. 2011; Van de Walle and Bouckaert 2003; West 2004).

Result of H3 shows that performance of government has a positive significant effect on citizens' satisfaction ($b = 0.996$, $t = 19.92$, ***), so H3 is supported. This finding is consistent with outcomes of the literature review (Morgeson et al. 2011; Van de Walle and Bouckaert 2003; West 2004).

To interpret the finding of H3, citizens perceive that real transformation of government results in improving the performance of the government and satisfied citizens. In practice, performance of government as perceived by citizens is related to the overall performance of the government and in particular efficiency and effectiveness of services provided to ordinary citizens. Furthermore, the performance of the government is linked to finding the needed information when needed and efficiency in completing transactions. Finally, it can be measured through looking at the values of public participation and engagement with government.

6.5.3.8 H4 Citizens' Satisfaction and Citizens' Trust and Confidence in Government

Citizens' trust and confidence is the dependent variable in this research. The literature suggests that citizens' trust and confidence enhances if citizens' are satisfied with the performance of government and its services (Bean 2015; Morgeson et al. 2011; Van de Walle and Bouckaert 2003).

Result of H4 shows that citizens' satisfaction has a positive significant effect on citizens' trust and confidence in government ($b = 0.963$, $t = 74.07$, ***), which support H4. This finding is consistent with outcomes of the literature review (Bean 2015; Van de Walle and Bouckaert 2003).

To interpret the finding of H4, citizens perceive that if they are satisfied and happy with the performance of government as well as its services, their trust and confidence in government improves. In practice, citizens' satisfaction is related to citizens' experience when using government services in general and in particular while completing government transactions. Furthermore, it is related with experience when using different channels used to deliver government services such as website, kiosk, mobile application, national call centres and social media.

Since trust and confidence is the dependent variable of this research, e-government, technology, citizens' expectations, transparency, accountability, transformation of government, performance of the government and citizens' satisfaction are the factors that influence citizens' trust and confidence in government.

6.5.4 Mediation Effects of Performance of Government and Citizens' Satisfaction

This research investigates the relationship between transformation of government and citizens' trust and confidence in government. This represents research questions Q3 and it has been discussed in details in the above sections. Based on the empirical findings of this research, transformation of government has a positive significant effect on citizens' trust and confidence in government. However, the relation between transformation of government and citizens' trust and confidence in government is mediated by performance of government and citizens' satisfaction.

Outcomes of the data analysis and in particular the path analysis is used to find out effects of both mediators. Table 5.15 shows that paths between (SATISF → TRU_COF), (PERFO → TRU_COF) and (TRANSF → TRU_COF) are all significant thereby indicating that both performance and satisfaction mediates partially between transformation and trust and confidence in government.

6.5.5 *Total Effects of All Relationships in the Conceptual Model*

Direct and indirect effects of all paths of the proposed conceptual model are presented in Sect. 5.12. The direct relationships have been covered under the above sections of this chapter. As for the indirect relationships, the first one that is not covered above is the relationship between transformation of government and citizens' satisfaction. The empirical finding shows that transformation of government has a positive significant effect on citizens' satisfaction. This is a natural effect taking into account that performance of government improved if real transformation of government exist (i.e. through improvements to the way government functions and delivers services as a result of fundamental changes implemented to the functions and processes of government). This in turn results in satisfied citizens. The results of the path analysis prove this assumption.

The second set of indirect effects are between the five factors of transformation of government: (a) e-government, (b) technology, (c) transparency, (d) accountability and (e) citizens' expectation on performance of government, citizens' satisfaction and citizens' trust and confidence in government. The results of the path analysis show that accountability, transparency and citizens' expectation respectively have indirect significant positive effects on performance of government, citizens' satisfaction and citizens' trust and confidence in government, whereas e-government and technology have indirect significant negative effects on performance of government, citizens' satisfaction and citizens' trust and confidence in government. It is interesting to know that the indirect positive and negative significant effects found here are exactly the same effects of e-government, technology, transparency, accountability and citizens' expectations on transformation of government, which were explained in details in the previous sections of this chapter.

To explain the above outcomes, it is useful to do a comparison between the literature and empirical findings of this research. The literature suggests that through being a true and successfully transformed government, performance of government improves, which leads to satisfied citizens with the government and its services. Moreover, citizens' trust and confidence improves if citizens' are satisfied with the performance of government and its services. The empirical findings are consistent with outcomes of the literature review. Based on this, the five factors of the transformation of government—e-government, technology, transparency, accountability and citizens' expectation should have the same effects on performance of government, citizens' satisfaction and citizens' trust and confidence in government.

From the above section, it is interesting to note that e-government and technology have negative indirect effects on performance of government, citizens' satisfaction and citizens' trust and confidence in government. The same reasons stated under H1a and H1b for explaining these negative effects can be applied here.

As explained before, these issues range from the newness of the e-government program in Bahrain to issues related to the adoption and diffusion of e-government systems and technical issues faced by the government in delivering integrated e-government systems.

6.6 Thoughts on the Empirical Findings

As discussed in the previous sections of this chapter, all suggested hypotheses for this research are confirmed by the empirical findings. The sequence and the flow of the findings can be summarised as follows. Real transformation of government (i.e. fundamental changes to the way core functions of government are performed to achieve noticeable gains in performance and efficiency) that takes into account e-government, technology, citizens' expectations, transparency and accountability - influences citizens' trust and confidence in government and is mediated by performance of government and citizens' satisfaction.

However, it was expected that the relationships between e-government and transformation of government as well as technology and transformation of government to be positively significant. The negative significant effects can be explained as: e-government and technology alone are not resulting in a real transformed government. Three other factors should be considered in any agenda for transforming government. It is clear from the empirical findings that citizens are considering the adoption of transparency by their government in all of its functions and activities as important, they also view the practice of accountability and listening to citizens' suggestions and concerns as very important in addition to e-government and technology.

6.7 Summary

The influence of transformation of government on citizens' trust and confidence in government was identified as the main gap of this research and as such, this research investigated this gap. Based on the outcome of the data analysis presented in chapter 5, this chapter discusses these findings and linking them to the literature as well as providing justifications and explanations from a practical perspective.

In doing so, an overview of the research was provided which included revisiting the related literature, reasons for conducting this research as well as its significance to knowledge and practice. Then, answers to the three research questions agreed for this research as well as results of the hypotheses testing were presented, linked to the literature, thoroughly discussed and justified taking into account that this research is based on citizens' perspective on all constructs and relations defined in the conceptual mode. It is worth pointing out that the empirical findings of this research are consistent with the outcomes of the literature review. Furthermore, all suggested hypotheses for this research are supported by the empirical findings.

One point to take into account by government and policy makers is that e-government and technology are not enough for achieving a successful transformed government and as such, other factors should be considered, which are, the adoption of transparency by government in all of its functions and activities, and practicing accountability and listening to citizens' suggestions and concerns. Finally, citizen's trust and confidence is positively influenced by real transformation of government.

The specific knowledge contributions and practical implications of this research are presented in Chap. 7.

References

Abu-Shanab E, Al-Azzam A (2012) Trust dimensions and the adoption of e-government in Jordan. Int J Inf Commun Technol Hum Dev (IJICTHD) 4(1):39–51

Al Rub S (2006) The impact of information technology on business performance management. The study of the Affairs Agency of Sudanese working abroad for the period (2000–2005). Master's Thesis, University of Science and Technology, Omdurman, Sudan

Alsaeed A, Adams C, Boakes R (2014) Challenges to the successful implementation of e-government initiatives in middle-east arabic countries and syria: literature review. In tGov workshop 14

Al-Shafi S, Weerakkody V (2008) The use of wireless internet parks to facilitate adoption and diffusion of e-government services: an empirical study in Qatar. AMCIS 2008 Proceedings, 322

Al-Sobhi F, Weerakkody V, Kamal MM (2010) An exploratory study on the role of intermediaries in delivering public services in Madinah City: case of Saudi Arabia. Transforming government. People, Process and Policy 4(1):14–36

Anthopoulos L, Reddick CG, Giannakidou I, Mavridis N (2016) Why e-government projects fail? An analysis of the Healthcare.gov website. Gov Inf Q 33(1):161–173

Bannister F, Connolly R (2011) Trust and transformational government: a proposed framework for research. Gov. Inf Q 28(2):137–147

Basu S (2004) E-government and developing countries: an overview. Int Rev Law, Comput & Technol 18(1):109–132

Bean C (2015) Changing citizen confidence: orientations towards political and social institutions in Australia, 1983–2010. The Open Polit Sci J 8(1):1–9

Bélanger F, Carter L (2008) Trust and risk in e-government adoption. J Strateg Inf Syst 17 (2):165–176

Bellamy C, Taylor J (1998) Governing in the information age. Open University Press, Buckingham, UK; Bristol, PA

Bingham LB (2010) Online deliberation and the United States open government initiative. Online Deliberation, 53

Bonham G, Seifert J, Thorson S (2001) The transformational potential of e-government: the role of political leadership. In 4th Pan European international relations conference, 8–11 September, 2001. University of Kent, UK

Bouckaert G, Van de Walle S, Kampen JK (2005) Potential for comparative public opinion research in public administration. Int Rev Admin Sci 71(2):229–240

Brown D (1999) Information systems for improved performance management: development approaches in US public agency. In: Heeks R (ed) Reinventing government in the information age. Routledge, New York, pp 321–330
Carter L, Bélanger F (2005) The utilization of e-government services: citizen trust, innovation and acceptance factors. Inf Syst J 15(1):5–25
Chen KC, Wei KC, Chen Z (2003) Disclosure, corporate governance, and the cost of equity capital: evidence from Asia's emerging markets. Corporate governance, and the cost of equity capital: evidence from Asia's emerging markets. Retrieved from http://dx.doi.org/10.2139/ssrn.422000
Choi H, Park MJ, Rho JJ, Zo H (2016) Rethinking the assessment of e-government implementation in developing countries from the perspective of the design–reality gap: applications in the Indonesian e-procurement system. Telecommun Policy 40(7):644–660
Colesca SE (2009) Understanding trust in e-government. Inzinerine Ekon-Eng Econ 3(3):7–15
Dalton RJ (2005) The social transformation of trust in government. Int Rev Sociol 15(1):133–154
Das Aundhe M, Das Aundhe M, Narasimhan R, Narasimhan R (2016) Public private partnership (PPP) outcomes in e-government–a social capital explanation. Int J Public Sector Manag 29(7):638–658
De Fine Licht J (2011) Do we really want to know? The potentially negative effect of transparency in decision making on perceived legitimacy. Scand Polit Stud 34(3), 183–201
Edwards M (2015) The trust deficit—concepts and causes of low public trust in governments. Committee of Experts on Public Administration, Fourteenth session, 20–24 April 2015, Item 3 of the provisional agenda
Fountain J (2001) Building the virtual state: information technology and institutional change. Brookings Institution Press, Washington, DC7
Giddens A (1984) The constitution of society. Polity Press, Cambridge
Graham M, Avery EJ (2013) Government public relations and social media: an analysis of the perceptions and trends of social media use at the local government level. Public Relat J 7 (4):1–21
Gray R, Owen DL, Maunders K (1987) Corporate social reporting: accounting and accountability. Hemel Hempstead, Herts, Prentice-Hall International
Grimmelikhuijsen S (2009) Do transparent government agencies strengthen trust? Inf Polity 14(3):173–186
Grimmelikhuijsen Stephan G (2012) A good man but a bad wizard: about the limits and future of transparency of democratic governments. Inf Polity 17(3–4):293–302
Grimmelikhuijsen S, Porumbescu G, Hong B, Im T (2013) The effect of transparency on trust in government: a cross-national comparative experiment. Public Adm Rev 73(4):575–586
Gunawong P, Gao P (2017) Understanding e-government failure in the developing country context: a process-oriented study. Inf Technol Dev 23(1):153–178
Hair JF, Anderson RE, Babin BJ, Black WC (2010) Multivariate data analysis: a global perspective, vol 7. Pearson, Upper Saddle River, NJ
Hameed S, Al-Shawabkah A (2013) Role of e-government in improving organizational performance in the civil status and passports department of Jordan. Developing Country Stud 3(5):50–64
Hanna N (2009) e-Transformation: enabling new development strategies. Springer Science & Business Media
Hood Christopher (2006) Beyond exchanging first principles? some closing comments. In: Hood Christopher, Heald David (eds) Transparency: the key to better governance?. Oxford University Press, Oxford, UK, pp 211–226
Huse M (2005) Accountability and creating accountability: a framework for exploring behavioural perspectives of corporate governance. Br J Manag 16(s1):S65–S79
International Labour Office (2015) World Employment and Social Outlook: Trends 2015. International Labour Organization
International Labour Office (2016) World Employment and Social Outlook: Trends 2016. International Labour Organization

International Labour Office (2017) World Employment and Social Outlook: Trends 2017. International Labour Organization
ISEA (1999) Accountability 1000. Institute of Social and Ethical Accountability, London
Kim S, Kim HJ, Lee H (2009) An institutional analysis of an e-government system for anti-corruption: the case of OPEN. Gov Inf Q 26(1):42–50
McNeal R, Hale K, Dotterweich L (2008) Citizen–government interaction and the Internet: expectations and accomplishments in contact, quality, and trust. J Inf Technol & Polit 5(2):213–229
Moon MJ, Norris DF (2005) Does managerial orientation matter? The adoption of reinventing government and e-government at the municipal level. Inf Syst J 15(1):43–60
Morgeson FV, Petrescu C (2011) Do they all perform alike? An examination of perceived performance, citizen satisfaction and trust with US federal agencies. Int Rev Admin Sci 77(3):451–479
Morgeson FV, VanAmburg D, Mithas S (2011) Misplaced trust? Exploring the structure of the e-government-citizen trust relationship. J Public Adm Res Theor 21(2):257–283
Mukhoryanova OA, Novikova IV, Rudich SB, Bogushevich EV (2016) E-government in the Western European Countries, Asia and in the USA. Indian J Sci Technol 9(16)
Nam T (2012) Citizens' attitudes toward open government and government 2.0. Int Rev Admin Sci 78(2):346–368
Navarrete C (2010) Trust in e-government transactional services: a study of citizens' perceptions in Mexico and the US. In 43rd Hawaii international conference on system sciences (HICSS), 2010. IEEE, pp. 1–10
Norquist G (2007) Transparency: the new democracy. Financial Times. Retrieved from www.ft.com/cms/s/2/2206f20c-45c9-11dc-b359-0000779fd2ac.html#axzz1CiOFLwDp
Northrup TA, Thorson SJ (2003) The web of governance and democratic accountability. Proceedings of the 36th annual Hawaii international conference on system sciences
O'Neill Onora (2002) A question of trust: the BBC Reith Lectures 2002. Cambridge University Press, Cambridge, UK
Office Cabinet (2005) Transformational government. Cabinet Office, London
Omar A, Weerakkody V, Sivarajah U (2017) Digitally enabled service transformation in UK public sector: a case analysis of universal credit. Int J Inf Manage 37(4):350–356
Pina V, Torres L, Royo S (2009) E-government evolution in EU local governments: a comparative perspective. Online Inf Rev 33(6):1137–1168
Roberts Alasdair (2006) Governmental adaptation to transparency rules. In: Hood Christopher, Heald David (eds) Transparency: the key to better governance?. Oxford University Press, Oxford, UK, pp 107–144
Robinson JP, Shaver PR, Wrightsman LS (1991) Criteria for scale selection and evaluation. Meas Pers Soc Psychol Attitudes 1(3):1–16
Roztocki N, Weistroffer HR (2016) Conceptualizing and researching the adoption of ICT andthe impact on socioeconomic development. Inf Technol Dev 22(4):541–549
Sehli H, Cooper V, Sarkar P (2016) The role of culture in developing the e-government absorptive capacity of agencies in Saudi Arabia: a conceptual model. PACIS 2016 Proceedings
Seifert JW, Chung J (2009) Using e-government to reinforce government—citizen relationships: comparing government reform in the United States and China. Soc Sci Comput Rev 27(1):3–23
Sekaran U (2000) Research Methods for Business: A Skill-building Approach. John Willey & Sons, USA
Song C, Lee J (2013) Can social media restore citizen trust in government? Public Manag Res Conf. Madison, WI, pp 20–22
Srivastava SC, Teo TS (2009) Citizen trust development for e-government adoption and usage: insights from young adults in Singapore. Communications of the Association for Information Systems. 25
Straub D, Boudreau MC, Gefen D (2004) Validation guidelines for IS positivist research. Commun Assoc Inf Syst 13:380–427

Teo TS, Srivastava SC, Jiang L (2008) Trust and electronic government success: an empirical study. J Manag Inf Syst 25(3):99–132
Tolbert CJ, Mossberger K (2006) The effects of e-government on trust and confidence in government. Public Adm Rev 66(3):354–369
United Nations (2012) E-government survey 2012: e-government for the people. Department of Economic and Social Affairs Division for Public Administration and Development Management
United Nations (2014) E-government survey 2014: e-government for the future we want. Department of Economic and Social Affairs Division for Public Administration and Development Management
United Nations (2016) E-government survey 2016: e-government in Support of Sustainable Development. Department of Economic and Social Affairs Division for Public Administration and Development Management
Van de Walle S, Bouckaert G (2003) Public service performance and trust in government: the problem of causality. Int J Public Adm 26(8–9):891–913
Van de Walle S, Van Roosbroek S, Bouckaert G (2008) Trust in the public sector: is there any evidence for a long-term decline? Int Rev Admin Sci 74(1):47–64
Waller P, Weerakkody V (2016) Digital government: overcoming the systemic failure of transformation. Working Paper 2. Brunel University, London
Al-Shafi S, Weerakkody, V. (2010) 'Factors affecting e-government adoption in the state of Qatar', *Proceedings of the European and Mediterranean Conference on Information Systems*, Abu Dhabi, UAE, 12–13 April 2010
Weerakkody V, Janssen M, Dwivedi Y (eds) (2009) Handbook of research on ICT enabled transformational government: a global perspective. Inf Sci Ref, Hershey, PA
Welch EW, Hinnant CC, Moon MJ (2005) Linking citizen satisfaction with e-government and trust in government. J Public Adm Res Theor 15(3):371–391
West DM (2004) E-government and the transformation of service delivery and citizen attitudes. Public Adm Rev 64(1):15–27
Williams PF (1987) The legitimate concern with fairness. Acc Organ Soc 12(2):169–189
World Bank (2017) Digital governance projects database. Available at https://data.worldbank.org/data-catalog/dg-projects-database
Zwahr T, Finger M, Müller P (2005) More than digitisation-the transformative potential of e-governance: an exploratory case study. In Proceedings of the 38th annual Hawaii international conference on system sciences, 2005, HICSS'05. IEEE, pp 127–127

Chapter 7
Conclusion

7.1 Introduction

Chapter 6 discussed the findings of this research and linked them to the literature as well as provided justifications and explanations for the findings from the practical perspective. In this chapter, the theoretical and practical contributions of this research are presented, limitations and future research are highlighted and finally the aim and objectives of this research are revisited.

This chapter is structured as follows. Section 7.2 provides an overview of the research in hand. This is followed by presenting the research contributions in Sect. 7.3. In Sect. 7.4, policy and practical implications are discussed. Then, in Sect. 7.5, limitations of the research are highlighted while providing a number of suggestions for future research in Sect. 7.6. The aim and objectives set out for this research in Chap. 1 are revisited and validated in Sect. 7.7. Personal experience and lessons learned from the Ph.D. journey are outlined in Sect. 7.8. Finally, a summary of the chapter is provided in Sect. 7.9.

7.2 Research Overview

The literature review exercise concluded that citizens' trust in their government has continued to decline during the last two decades (Bean 2015; Edwards 2015; Teo et al. 2008; Morgeson et al. 2011; World Employment and Social Outlook Trends 2015, 2016, 2017). In the literature, e-government was viewed as a solution to reverse this decline (see for example Morgeson et al. 2011; Teo et al. 2008; Tolbert and Mossberger 2006). A number of e-government projects and solutions were deployed and implemented around the globe for which a large sum of money has been spent as showed in Table 6.1 of this thesis. Unfortunately, many of the e-government projects failed and did not meet the expected results. Citizens' trust

M. Mahmood, *Does Digital Transformation of Government Lead to Enhanced Citizens' Trust and Confidence in Government?*, Springer Theses,
https://doi.org/10.1007/978-3-030-01759-0_7

and confidence on the other hand has continued to decline (Welch et al. 2005; Bannister and Connolly 2011; Kim et al. 2009; Morgeson et al. 2011; Weerakkody et al. 2009). In investigating the phenomena of the decline in citizens' trust and confidence in government, digital or ICT enabled transformation of government was found to have the potential to reverse this decline through fundamental changes to the way core functions of government are performed to achieve noticeable gains in performance and efficiency (Bannister and Connolly 2011; Waller and Weerakkody 2016; Zwahr et al. 2005). From reviewing the literature, it can be concluded that there is a gap in the literature, which is a lack of studies that investigated the relationship and influence of transformation of government on citizens' trust and confidence in government.

In addition to e-government and transformation of government, other factors have been identified in the literature that influence citizens' trust and confidence, such as, technology (Morgeson et al. 2011; Tolbert and Mossberger 2006), transparency (Bannister and Connolly 2011; Kim et al. 2009), accountability (Bannister and Connolly 2011; Kim et al. 2009), citizens' expectations (Morgeson and Petrescu 2011; Morgeson et al. 2011), government performance (Bouckaert et al. 2005; Morgeson et al. 2011; Van de Walle and Bouckaert 2003; Van de Walle et al. 2008) and citizens' satisfactions (Bouckaert et al. 2005; Morgeson et al. 2011; Teo et al. 2008; Van de Walle and Bouckaert 2003; Van de Walle et al. 2008). However, there is no comprehensive research that has investigated these factors in detail nor agreed on a set of common factors that contribute to the decline in citizens' trust and confidence in government (Bannister and Connolly 2011; West 2004). Many of the previous studies have largely focused on technical, service quality, usability and adoption aspects of ICT enabled transformation projects in government with limited impact on practice. In other words, most prior studies have focused on e-government systems and citizen facing aspects and largely ignored the policy issues that trigger transformation together with the broader issues of change that is needed within the transformation agenda. Therefore, there is a gap in research to gain a deeper insight into the decline in citizens' trust and confidence in government and its relationship with digital transformation of government.

As such, the aim of this research was to investigate the influence of digital transformation of government on citizens' trust and confidence in government. Furthermore, effects of other factors on this phenomenon were also investigated in this research. Bahrain as part of the GCC countries was selected for conducting this research as it is the most advanced country in e-government development and implementation as per the United National Surveys of 2012, 2014 and 2016. Moreover, the demographic make-up of the country, the support for e-government from its government (around $106 million, has been allocated for digital government initiatives in Bahrain since the inception of the e-government initiative in 2007), and the e-participation related challenges currently faced in Bahrain (United Nations E-Government Survey 2014, 2016) as well as the lack of studies conducted in Bahrain that investigated the relationship between transformation efforts in government and citizens' trust in government provided the rationale for selecting Bahrain as the empirical context for this study. In order to achieve the aim of this research, three research questions were posited which were: (1) what factors influence transformation of government, (2) how these factors influence transformation of government, and (3) how transformation of government can be related to trust and confidence in citizens.

Chapter 1 included much of the above sections as a background and motivation for conducting this research. Furthermore, it included the aim, objectives, research questions and research hypotheses suggested for this research.

The outcomes of the literature review are covered in Chap. 2, which was conducted using mainly normative and secondary sources as well as a few primary case study sources. This stage helped in confirming and synthesising the research problem, gaps and questions as well as research aim and objectives. Moreover, key factors influencing transformation of government and trust and confidence in government were been identified and discussed in details along with supporting theories for each.

The developed conceptual model for this research was illustrated and described in Chap. 3. The conceptual model was influenced by the model developed by Morgeson et al. (2011) and factors identified during the literature review phase. Additionally, the research hypotheses were suggested along with the supporting theories for every defined construct and relationship within the conceptual mode as well as the base theory that supports the conceptual model.

The research design and approach was defined and presented in Chap. 4. Positivism was selected as a research philosophy and explanatory as a research purpose as it best suited the aim and objectives of this research. Accordingly, a quantitative methodology was employed for this research. The target audiences which are ordinary citizens living in Bahrain were approached randomly through the development and distribution of an online survey through different means such as email, SMS and social media applications. Prior to launching the main survey, pre-test and pilot test were performed to validate the conceptual model and hypotheses as well as to ensure the data collected during the pilot test was reliable.

Data analysis of the collected data was presented in Chap. 5. SEM was chosen as a multivariate technique for this research to validate the fitness of the conceptual model and test the hypotheses through performing CFA and path analysis. Before performing CFA and path analysis, a number of tests were conducted to prepare a clean data for the SEM, which included reliability and validity of the research instrument, correlation and normality of the data distribution.

In Chap. 6, the findings of the data analysis was discussed. It mapped the findings of the research to the gap identified and the three questions agreed for this research. The outcomes of the empirical findings of this research were found to be consistent with the literature review. Moreover, answers to the three research questions and results of the eight hypotheses were thoroughly discussed, justified, explained and linked to the practical side. It is interesting to find out that e-government and technology are not sufficient for achieving a true transformed government. Three other factors should also be considered, which are citizens' expectations, demonstration of transparency and practice of accountability.

7.3 Theoretical Contributions

Contents and outcomes of this research synthesised the information system literature and in particular the areas of ICT or digital enabled transformation of government and citizens' trust and confidence in government. The sections below present a number of important contributions to the existing literature and the growing body of knowledge related to important concepts.

7.3.1 Contribution 1

As far as the researcher's knowledge, this research is first of its type that investigates from citizens' perspective the relationship between transformation and citizens' trust and confidence in government. Therefore, this research is considered as a novel contribution to the body of existing knowledge.

7.3.2 Contribution 2

The main gap found for this research was the lack of knowledge on how digital transformation of government influences citizens' trust and confidence in government. As such, the aim agreed for this research was in line with the identified gap. To address this aim and gap, research question Q3 was posited. As per the outcomes of the empirical results, transformation of government has a positive significant effect on citizens' trust and confidence mediated by performance of government and citizens' satisfaction.

7.3.3 Contribution 3

Apart from transformation of government, other factors have been discussed in the literature to understand the phenomena of the decline in citizens' trust and confidence in government. However, no common set of factors have been discussed comprehensively in the literature. To address this, outcomes of this research showed that e-government, technology, citizens' expectations, transparency, accountability, performance of the government and citizens' satisfaction are the main factors that influence citizens' trust and confidence in government. Moreover, the research illustrated how these factors are influencing citizens' trust and confidence in government as well as how they are related and linked with each other. This is visible in the developed conceptual model as well as Sect. 6.5.5 of this thesis, which shows the total effects of all paths in the conceptual model.

7.3.4 Contribution 4

Since the aim of this research was to investigate the influence of digital transformation of government on citizens' trust and confidence in government, the same arguments placed above for a need to define a common set of factors influencing citizens' trust and confidence in government, apply to the transformation of government. To address this, research question Q1 was posited. As per the outcomes of this research, e-government, technology, citizens' expectations, transparency and accountability were found to effect transformation of government. Furthermore, the research illustrated how these five factors influence transformation of government, which answer research question Q2 posited for this research. Out of these five factors, three were found to have positive influence on transformation of government, which are citizens' expectations, transparency and accountability. As for the remaining factors, which are e-government and technology, they were found to have negative effect on transformation of government. As per the literature, the term "transformation of government" is a complex one and it is hard to find a common definition for it (Bannister and Connolly 2011; West 2004). The findings of this research, add to the current knowledge a better understanding of the definition of "transformation of government" and the role of transparency, accountability, technology, citizens' expectations and e-government within this context.

7.3.5 Contribution 5

The findings of the research show that transformation of government is positively influencing citizens' trust and confidence in government mediated by the performance of the government and citizens' satisfaction. The indirect relationships between performance of the government and citizens' trust and confidence in government and the direct relationship between citizens' satisfaction and citizens' trust and confidence in government were found to have positive significant effects respectively. Similarly, transformation of government was found to have an indirect positive significant effect on citizens' trust and confidence in government. This indicates that both performance and satisfaction mediates partially between transformation and trust and confidence in government. In other words, transformation of government positively influences citizens' trust and confidence in government with or without mediators. This finding addresses the research gap by reconfirming that transformation of government positively influences citizens' trust and confidence in government, which helps in advancing the understanding of the relationship between transformation of government and citizens' trust and confidence in government.

7.3.6 Contribution 6

This research found that e-government and technology are not enough for achieving a successful transformation of government, and improving the performance of government, or enhancing citizens' satisfaction and reversing the decline in citizens' trust and confidence in government. Other factors should be considered in this equation, which are adoption of transparency by the government in all of its functions and activities, practicing accountability and managing and meeting citizens' expectations and demands. Although the concepts of transparency and accountability have been discussed in many studies and are established as key components of e-government, their influence on citizens' perception of government has not been empirically tested in the context of transformation of government and citizens' trust and confidence in government.

7.3.7 Contribution 7

In order to fulfil the aim agreed for this research as well as to answer the three research questions, a conceptual model was developed, tested and validated. The conceptual model consisted of nine constructs, eight hypotheses and two mediators. This bridges the gap found in literature, which revealed an absence of theoretical models associated with 'transformation of government' and citizens' trust and confidence in government. As far as the research's knowledge, this is the first conceptual model of its type that investigates the relationship between transformation of government and citizens' trust and confidence in government.

7.3.8 Contribution 8

The conceptual model was supported and validated by suitable theories whether it is the base theory for the whole model or theories supporting the proposed relationships in the model. The base theory in this research, Exit Voice theory, confirmed the relationship between transformation of government and citizens' trust and confidence in government. As far as the researcher's knowledge, this is the first time Exit-Voice Theory is used in the context of investigating transformation of government and citizens' trust and confidence in government. The majority of the previous studies conducted in the area of e-government mainly focused on user adoption theories (example Technology Acceptance Model, TAM; Diffusion of Innovation, DOI). Only one study (Morgeson et al. 2011) covered exit voice theory but again in the context of e-government and its relationship on citizens' trust and confidence in government.

7.3.9 Contribution 9

The use of quantitative research methodology along with email, SMS and social media applications—for distribution randomly—an online survey to ordinary citizens living in Bahrain is considered as a contribution of this research taking into account that this is the first study of its type as per the researcher's knowledge within Bahrain. As for generalising the findings of this research, the use of the quantitative research methodology supports the generalisation of the findings to some extent within the context of GCC countries due to their shared values, cultures and political structures (Bryman 2004; Creswell 2003).

7.3.10 Contribution 10

In the context of this research, the use of SEM and AMOS as statistical tools for data analysis and in particular for conducting CFA and path analysis is considered as a contribution considering that this is the first study of its type as per the researcher's knowledge that investigated the relationship between transformation of government and citizens' trust and confidence in government; this sets the path for similar studies in future.

The knowledge gained from the contributions stated above help in better understanding the decline in citizens' trust and confidence in government, advancing the understanding of the relationship between transformation of government and citizens' trust, and confidence in government.

7.4 Policy and Practice Implications

Since this research is based on citizens' perspective, outcomes of this research ultimately benefit citizens in terms of government managing and meeting their expectations and demands, improving citizens' satisfaction and finally gaining and retaining citizens' trust and confidence in the government.

From citizens' perspective, the findings of this research confirm that transformation of government plays a main role in improving citizens' trust and confidence in government as well as enhancing citizens' engagement with government and its services. Furthermore, the research offers a set of factors that help the policy makers, practitioners and concerned agencies in better understanding citizens' trust and confidence in the government as well as transformation of government along with the effect of each factor on both concepts and how these factors are related with each other. Factors influencing citizens' trust and confidence in government are e-government, technology, citizens' expectations, transparency, accountability, transformation of government, performance of the government and citizens' satisfaction. As for transformation of government, the factors are e-government, technology, citizens' expectations, transparency and accountability.

The conceptual model developed for this study illustrates the two concepts, transformation of government and citizens' trust and confidence in government, and relationships between both factors influence each. The conceptual model can be used as a frame of reference for both the policy makers and researchers for better understanding the phenomena of the decline in citizens' trust and confidence in government as well as the role of transformation in reversing this decline. Furthermore, the conceptual model can be used as a predicting or forecasting tool that can be used by policy makers and practitioners for predicting citizens' behaviour in terms of expectations, satisfactions and trust and confidence in government and its services.

The policy makers should take note of the fact that development and implementation of e-government system in the country is not enough and sufficient for achieving true, real and successful transformation of government (i.e. that result in fundamental changes to the structure, functions and core processes of government) nor enhance citizens' trust and confidence in government. The same argument applies to technology used by government agencies for the provisioning of their own services or integrating with the concerned government agencies to provided digital government services. Other factors should work together with e-government and technology, which are meeting citizens' expectations, adopting transparency and practicing accountability at all levels of government. In practice, this means that governments need to accept new ideas for implementing the desired changes that will lead to real transformation and high-level officials in government should be eager to do things differently, and be flexible in adopting where procedures need changing to meet new conditions and solve problems as they arise. They also need to be willing to practice transparency in all functions and activities of government, be accountable for their conduct, and willing to listen to citizens' needs.

Reflecting on the significant negative effects of e-government and technology on transformation of government, performance of the government, citizens' satisfaction and citizens' trust and confidence in government, the government and policy makers should acknowledge the fact that more need to done on both factors so as to minimise the negative impact of challenges such as skills needed to use e-government services, trust in e-government platforms, security and privacy concerns, enhance citizens' interest and awareness in e-government. Other issues that may need attention include training and education for citizens to use e-government systems, better integration amongst government agencies to provide one-stop services to citizens.

The findings of the research highlighted other challenges under each construct of this research. Starting with citizens' expectations, the key challenges are provisioning of services at the time promised by the government, offering prompt services, readiness of the government to respond to citizens' queries, government officials pay attention to citizens' needs and have the knowledge to answer citizens' questions, citizens feel safe and confident when they perform their online transactions, government informing citizens in advance of any changes to the services and the government maintaining error-free-records.

As for transparency, the research identified the following challenges. Dissemination of government related information such as processes, procedures, services, tracking applications, activities, transactions, policies, decisions, regulations and legal instruments. Commissioning consultation processes with the stakeholders is considered as a key issue to be addressed by the government. On the other hand, accountability exist when government provides justifications for its conduct, availability of appeals and escalations processes and usage of budgets properly and in an authorized manner.

Challenges identified for performance of the government revolve around the overall perception of the performance of the government and in particular efficiency and effectiveness of services provided to ordinary citizens. Furthermore, finding the needed information and efficiency in completing transactions. Finally, level of public participation and engagement with government is important. Citizens' satisfaction on the other hand is related to citizens' experience when using government services in general and in particular while completing government services transactions. Furthermore, it is related with experience when using different channels used to deliver government services such as website, kiosk, mobile application, national call centres and social media.

Moving away from challenges presented in the above sections to the area of policy implications, the government should accept and acknowledge the complexity of the phenomenon related to transformation of government and citizens' trust and confidence in government. In doing so, any government policy should address and overcome at least the challenges mentioned above. In particular, the government should discard the idea that adoption of e-government along with equipping the government with latest technologies result in real and successful transformation of government as well as enhancing citizens' trust and confidence in government. Instead, it should consider all factors stated above in any policy it wishes to release related to the same. For this, well-coordinated efforts are needed to take place between different arms of policy makers in the country.

Despite the advanced stages of e-government implementation in Bahrain, the policy makers should consider transformation of government along with all factors influencing it carefully so that it results in a real and successful transformed government (i.e. through fundamental changes to structure, functions and processes), which has the potential to enhance citizens' trust and confidence in government even more. Huge investments have been made on e-government initiatives in Bahrain since its inception; the e-government budget represents around 23% of the overall ICT budget on a yearly basis (Frost and Sullivan, March 2017). As such, and in order to avoid any failures in e-government and associated transformation initiatives (as illustrated in Tables 6.1 and 6.2 of this thesis), the results of this research offer many suggestions for government and policy makers in Bahrain in particular (and others) to consider.

One way to implement the above is through preparation and issuance of a national policy for transformation of government where all factors highlighted in this research are included and solutions are offered for the potential challenges that may hinder shifting to a true transformed government. A proper strategic management framework along with clear targets and Key Performance Indicators should be in place to ensure the successful development and implementation of the national policy for transformation of government. Since this is a big and critical initiative for the country, coordinated efforts need to take place amongst all concerned parties in government. Another way for enabling a real transformation of government is to effectively utilise and observe ICT instruments used to implement and deliver new policies (Waller and Weerakkody 2016).

The above sections highlighted some implications for policy and practice as well as offering a number of suggestions for policy makers and practitioners. In detail, it provides an overview of the broader dimensions of the subject in hand and understanding of the critical factors influencing citizens' trust and confidence in government and finally, the effect of transformation of government on citizens' trust and confidence in government.

7.5 Research Limitations

Every research has limitations and the same applies for the research in hand. The sections below present limitations encountered in this research.

The influence of other factors such as cultural and social on citizens' trust and confidence in government as well as transformation of government were neither included within the identified factors for this research nor the developed conceptual model. These two concepts are sensitive and critical that need in depth understanding and investigation and due to the time constraints of the research in hand, they were not covered.

Findings of this research are only based on citizens' perspective on every construct and relationship defined within the conceptual model. Other perspectives such as governmental, business, or non-governmental organisations are not covered in this research.

The online survey was randomly distributed to ordinary citizens living in Bahrain through email, SMS and social media and as such, it appears that the majority of respondents were internet users and were well educated, which may result in a bias of the results to a certain direction. Although the online survey was shared with citizens from different areas of Bahrain and different groups, which span over a variety of professions and backgrounds, still there is a risk that the sample was drawn from a self-selecting one. As far as the researcher's knowledge and best efforts in distributing the survey across Bahrain, the collected sample represents a good demographic mix.

The research methodology adopted for this research was quantitative. Although it can be supportive for generalisation of the findings, this may restrict the ability of the research to obtain an in-depth view of factors influencing citizens' trust and confidence in government as well as transformation of government from citizens, government and third party perspectives. The researcher was unable to employ a hybrid/mixed methodology due to time constraints of the research in hand.

Although outcomes of the research is particularly applicable to the specific situation and conditions of the place where this study was conducted, Bahrain, generalisation within the GCC region is fair as most countries share the same political, economic and culture structure. Finally, the United Nations Surveys released in 2012, 2014 and 2016 consider Bahrain in the same basket as other GCC countries in terms of the development and implementation of e-government systems. Generalization beyond the GCC region may be difficult and as such, careful attention should be given to the differences in political, economic, culture and ICT structures when interpreting the outcomes of this study in other national and/or regional contexts.

Moderation effect was not covered in this research, which might have provided further explanations and analysis of impacts of factors such as gender, age, income education level and nationality on the relationship between transformation of government and citizens' trust and confidence in government.

The limitations pointed out above provide paths for future research, which will enrich and synthesize the information system literature and in particular the areas of transformation of government and citizens' trust and confidence in government.

7.6 Future Research

Deriving from the above limitations, this research offers a number of suggestions for future research that may result in enriching and strengthening this research.

As mentioned under the limitations section, cultural and social concepts may play an important role in the context of this study (Bannister and Connolly 2011; Bertot et al. 2010; Dalton 2005; Van de Walle and Bouckaert 2003). Therefore, future research may investigate their influence on both transformation of government and citizens' trust and confidence in government. The conceptual model can thus be expanded to include cultural and social and then link them to the existing factors as suitable.

To ensure non-internet users are covered in this research and avoid the risk of self-selecting the respondents and data obtained from a large and diversified population living in Bahrain, delivery and collection of questionnaire could have been used in parallel to the online survey (Saunders 2011). Additionally, increasing the sampling size may overcome any potential bias in the results towards a certain direction.

To confirm the findings and to obtain an in-depth view of factors influencing citizens' trust and confidence in government as well as transformation of government, a qualitative research methodology through conducting in depth interviews and using focus groups techniques with citizens' and citizens' representatives could have enriched this study.

This research can be conducted in another country in the GCC region or any other country in different parts of the world. Moreover, since all GCC countries share almost the same political, economic, culture and ICT structures, it will be interesting to conduct a comparative analysis of the GCC countries related to the same subject. Going beyond the GCC region, other regions can replicate similar research.

As mentioned previously, this study is based on citizens' perceptions on all constructs and relationships defined and covered within the conceptual model. Therefore, a future study may cover governmental and political perspectives. Gender, age, income education level and nationality may be used as moderators in any future research, which will clarify the role and influence of such control variables on the findings.

Policy aspects of government such as the core functions of government, processes, procedures, policy/regulations/legal instruments and decision making processes (Bannister and Connolly 2011; O'Neill 2009; Waller and Weerakkody 2016) in presence of factors such as transformation of government, technology and e-government can also be covered in a future research.

Finally, conducting longitudinal studies along with combining both qualitative and quantitative methods help tremendously in deep understanding of the impact of transformation on citizens' trust and confidence in government.

7.7 Revisiting the Aim and Objectives of the Research

As explained previously, the aim of this research was to investigate the relationship between transformation of government and citizens' trust and confidence as dependent variable. In order to achieve the aim of this research, a number of objectives were defined as explained in Chap. 1 which are achieved as discussed in different chapters of this thesis. Table 7.1 below illustrates the five research objectives, indicating whether each objective is met or not and finally providing a summary on how each objective is accomplished during the different phases of the research along with mapping into related chapters of the thesis.

Table 7.1 Meeting the aim and objectives of the research

#	Research objective	Status	Chapter	Summary of how the objective was accomplished
1	Examining the current literature with regard to factors influencing transformation of government and understand the relationship that exists between those factors and transformation of government	Met	1,2	Chapter 2 identified and discussed all factors affecting citizens' trust and confidence in government including transformation of government. Moreover, Chap. 2 identified and discussed five factors that are affecting transformation of government, how these factors are influencing transformation and how these factors are working collectively

(continued)

Table 7.1 (continued)

#	Research objective	Status	Chapter	Summary of how the objective was accomplished
2	In a similar vein, studying the extant literature and reviewing the theories and models that could be used to understand the concepts of transformation of government and citizens' trust and confidence as well examining the relationship between the two concepts through proposing a conceptual model and hypotheses	Met	2,3	Chapters 2 and 3 presented and discussed the different theories and models that are supporting the concepts covered in this research as well as the potential relationship between transformation of government and citizens' trust and confidence in government. This include, the relationships between factors influencing transformation of government and transformation of government as well as transformation of government and citizens' trust and confidence mediated by performance of the government and citizens' satisfactions A conceptual model was developed using the model developed by Morgeson et al. (2011) as a base model and taking into account the factors identified during the literature review phase. The defined constructs and relationships within the conceptual model were supported by appropriate theories as pointed out above As for hypotheses, eight hypotheses were proposed for this research
3	Defining the methodological framework for conducting empirical research to test the proposed hypotheses	Met	4	Quantitative methodology was adopted for this research along with an online survey targeting randomly ordinary citizens of the Kingdom of Bahrain through using email, SMS and social media applications. In order to validate the conceptual model and ensure reliability of the data, a pilot survey was conducted prior conducting the main survey

(continued)

Table 7.1 (continued)

#	Research objective	Status	Chapter	Summary of how the objective was accomplished
4	Analysing the empirical finding and highlighting the key relationships between the different constructs proposed in the conceptual model	Met	5	SPSS along with AMOS was used in this research for the data analysis. The SEM was employed for this research as multivariate analysis technique. CFA and path analysis were performed which resulted in a good fit of the proposed conceptual model and supporting all hypotheses set for this research. The findings of the research confirm that the model functions well
5	Discussing the key findings in relation to the literature, outlining the main theoretical and practical implications of the study and offering suggestions for future research	Met	6,7	All findings were presented, discussed and mapped with the research questions and hypotheses suggested for the research. A number of theoretical contributions and practical implications were presented and discussed. The key one is that as per the researcher's knowledge this is the first study of its type that investigates the relationship between transformation of government and citizens' trust and confidence in government. Furthermore, the proposed model also makes a novel contribution at a conceptual level for the relationship between transformation of government and citizens' trust and confidence in government

7.8 Personal Experience and Lessons Learned from the Ph.D. Journey

Before concluding this chapter, it is fit to share the experience that the researcher went through so far as well as a number of lessons learned that might be useful for current and future researchers.

In the beginning, it is worth highlighting that the Ph.D. journey is a very challenging one and can be compared to bungee jumping. It includes professional work and all kinds of emotions and feelings such as fear from the unknown, stress, energetic, enthusiasm, working hard, disappointment, excitement, accomplishment and the desire to break through tough challenges. The Ph.D. project in hand was a real challenge for the researcher taking into account that he is practitioner who has over 18 years of experience in industry and the move from industry and business to an academic field/environment was a tough one.

The key message out of the Ph.D. journey is the systematic process to be followed by researchers for conducting and accomplishing different phases of research; through following this process, any research can be conducted smoothly. The scope of this research was bounded by the time specified to complete and submit the thesis; otherwise, many items could have been expanded on or new tasks could have been included within the scope of the study. For example, other factors such as cultural and social could have been included in the research and subsequently in the proposed conceptual model. Moreover, a comparative study could have been conducted amongst the GCC countries since all share a common culture and have a similar ICT environment. As for the research methodology, a qualitative approach along with interviews and focus groups could have been used for the purposes of confirming and validating the findings of the quantitative approach as well as ensuring non-internet users were covered.

Although the target audience of this research were ordinary citizens living in Bahrain, responding to the online survey was a real and hard challenge. Despite the large number of personal contacts, the researcher has in Bahrain and using social media, only 313 completed responses were received; in fact, the researcher expected over 1000 responses. Apart from the unexpected number of responses, conducting data analysis using tools such as SPSS and AMOS was another difficulty. In future, dedicated sessions provided by the academic institute on how to use SPSS and AMOS at the early stages of the Ph.D. journey would be very helpful and useful. Following over 18 years of experience in the industry and with little knowledge about academia, the researcher faced another challenge on adopting an academic writing style particularly during the early stages of the research. This was gradually overcome by writing conference papers, converting these to journals and constantly discussing research with the supervisory team. The way of thinking as an academic was a completely different experience, in particular having to justify and refer to the literature when proposing ideas or arguments. Finally, priorities in life as well as time management are the most important elements that should be considered carefully by any researcher. The researcher had completely changed his lifestyle and abandoned many hobbies and activities to accommodate the Ph.D. journey.

The researcher has benefited a lot from publishing conference papers and journal articles as well as actively participating in academic events in different parts of the world. The critical feedback received as part of the process to publish a conference paper and journal articles helped a lot in improving the academic writing skills and way of thinking. In addition to the publications, the relationship with the academic supervisors is a very important one for completing safely the Ph.D. journey. In addition to the regular skype and phone calls, the researcher met his academic supervisor in many countries around the world such as the UK, USA, Bahrain and

Qatar for only one purpose, that is to have intellectual discussions about the research at hand and receive critical feedback on the content of the research. When the researcher started his Ph.D. journey, no plan was there to publish or even think of publishing papers. However, the academic supervisor smartly encouraged and pushed the researcher to publish over 10 conference and journal papers at the end of his Ph.D. journey.

Despite the above challenges and difficulties, starting this Ph.D. journey was a personal choice and the researcher had to navigate through the ups and down of this path. Personally, the Ph.D. journey was an exciting experience and unique one as well as being a fruitful and eventful one.

7.9 Summary

This research investigated the relationship between transformation of government and citizens' trust and confidence in government. Findings of this research were presented and discussed in the previous chapter. This chapter identified a number of research contributions as well as practical implications to policy makers and practitioners. The research limitations and suggestions for future research were presented and discussed.

As far as the researcher's knowledge, this research is first of its type that investigates from citizens' perspective the relationship between transformation and citizens' trust and confidence in government. In doing so, a conceptual model developed for this research was tested, validated and proven functioning well. Again, as far as the researcher's knowledge, this is the first conceptual model of its type that investigates the relationship between the same concepts mentioned above. Therefore, this research is considered as a novel contribution to the body of knowledge.

Finally, the five objectives identified for this research were accomplished successfully and this means the aim of this research was successfully achieved.

References

Bannister F, Connolly R (2011) Trust and transformational government: a proposed framework for research. Gov Info Q 28(2):137–147

Bean C (2015) Changing citizen confidence: orientations towards political and social institutions in Australia, 1983–2010. The Open Polit Sci J 8(1):1–9

Bertot JC, Jaeger PT, Grimes JM (2010) Using ICTs to create a culture of transparency: E-government and social media as openness and anti-corruption tools for societies. Gov Inf Q 27(3):264–271

Bouckaert G, Van de Walle S, Kampen JK (2005) Potential for comparative public opinion research in public administration. Int Rev Adm Sci 71(2):229–240

Bryman A (2004) Social research methods, 2nd edn. Oxford University Press, Oxford

Creswell JW (2003) Research design: quantitative, qualitative, and mixed methods approaches. Sage Publication Inc., Thousand Oaks
Dalton RJ (2005) The social transformation of trust in government. Int Rev Sociol 15(1):133–154
Edwards M (2015) The trust deficit—concepts and causes of low public trust in governments. Committee of Experts on Public Administration, Fourteenth session, 20–24 April 2015, Item 3 of the provisional agenda
International Labour Office (2015) World employment and social outlook: trends 2015. International Labour Organization
International Labour Office (2016) World employment and social outlook: trends 2016. International Labour Organization
International Labour Office (2017) World employment and social outlook: trends 2017. International Labour Organization
Kim S, Kim HJ, Lee H (2009) An institutional analysis of an e-government system for anti-corruption: the case of OPEN. Gov Info Q 26(1):42–50
Morgeson FV, Petrescu C (2011) Do they all perform alike? An examination of perceived performance, citizen satisfaction and trust with US federal agencies. Int Rev Adm Sci 77 (3):451–479
Morgeson FV, VanAmburg D, Mithas S (2011) Misplaced trust? Exploring the structure of the e-government-citizen trust relationship. J Public Adm Res Theor 21(2):257–283
O'Neill R (2009) The transformative impact of E-Government on public governance in New Zealand. Public Manag Rev 11(6):751–770
Saunders MN (2011) Research methods for business students. 5/e. Pearson Education India
Teo TS, Srivastava SC, Jiang L (2008) Trust and electronic government success: an empirical study. J Manage Info Syst 25(3):99–132
Tolbert CJ, Mossberger K (2006) The effects of E-Government on trust and confidence in government. Public Adm Rev 66(3):354–369
United Nations (2012) E-government survey 2012: e-government for the people. Department of Economic and Social Affairs Division for Public Administration and Development Management
United Nations (2014) E-government survey 2014: e-government for the future we want. Department of Economic and Social Affairs Division for Public Administration and Development Management
United Nations (2016) E-government survey 2016: e-government in Support of Sustainable Development. Department of Economic and Social Affairs Division for Public Administration and Development Management
Van de Walle S, Bouckaert G (2003) Public service performance and trust in government: the problem of causality. Int J Public Adm 26(8–9):891–913
Van de Walle S, Van Roosbroek S, Bouckaert G (2008) Trust in the public sector: is there any evidence for a long-term decline? Int Rev Adm Sci 74(1):47–64
Waller P, Weerakkody V (2016) Digital government: overcoming the systemic failure of transformation. Working Paper 2. Brunel University, London
Weerakkody V, Janssen M, Dwivedi Y (eds) (2009) Handbook of research on ICT enabled transformational government: a global perspective. Info Sci Ref, Hershey, PA
Welch EW, Hinnant CC, Moon MJ (2005) Linking citizen satisfaction with e-government and trust in government. J Public Adm Res Theor 15(3):371–391
West DM (2004) E-Government and the transformation of service delivery and citizen attitudes. Public Adm Rev 64(1):15–27
Zwahr T, Finger M, Müller P (2005) More than digitisation-the transformative potential of e-governance: an exploratory case study. In: Proceedings of the 38th annual Hawaii international conference on System sciences, 2005, HICSS'05, IEEE, pp. 127–127

Appendix A
Research Instruments (Pilot Survey)

Construct	No.	Questions
EGOV	Q1	People would learn to use the website very quickly
	Q2	I found information on the website to be very useful
	Q3	I found helpful features on the website for accomplishing my task
	Q4	Through every step of navigation through the website, I found the website to consistently provide useful information
	Q5	I found that the content in the website was organized appropriately
	Q6	I found the design of the website visually pleasing
	Q7	I found that various functions within the government department were properly not linked together (R)
	Q8	I was able to save the transaction details for future reference
	Q9	I was able to choose the manner in which I am sent reminders/notifications about my transaction
	Q10	I was able to request information the way I wanted (i.e. on mobile devices or electronic mail) on the days I wanted to
TRANSPY	Q11	The government departments' programs are implemented more transparently in the website
	Q12	The government departments' decision making is transparently disclosed in the website
	Q13	The citizen can clearly see the progress and situation of the decision making through the website
	Q14	The government departments' policies are seldom disclosed transparently on the website (R)
	Q15	The government departments' website discloses sufficient and reliable information to the citizen on its policies

(continued)

M. Mahmood, *Does Digital Transformation of Government Lead to Enhanced Citizens' Trust and Confidence in Government?*, Springer Theses,
https://doi.org/10.1007/978-3-030-01759-0

(continued)

Construct	No.	Questions
ACOUNT	Q16	The government departments recognise their responsibilities towards all communities
	Q17	The government departments do not set clear operating goals to be achieved (R)
	Q18	The government departments maintain detailed and up-to-date records
	Q19	The government departments foster collaboration with other related agencies
	Q20	The government departments ensure funds are used properly and in an authorized manner
TECH	Q21	The government departments use computer networks to connect all of its divisions
	Q22	The government departments are keen on providing network security in order to secure the information
	Q23	Data exchange is conducted with great ease among the government departments' divisions through the available means of communication
EXPEC	Q24	Government departments show sincere interest in solving citizens' problems
	Q25	Government departments provide services at the time promised
	Q26	Government departments maintain error-free records
	Q27	Government departments inform citizens when services will be performed
	Q28	Government departments offer prompt services to citizens
	Q29	Government departments sometimes are not willing to help citizens (R)
	Q30	Government departments readily respond to citizens' request
	Q31	Government departments able to instill confidence in citizens
	Q32	Government departments ensure that citizens feel safe in their transactions
	Q33	Government departments fail to ensure that employees are courteous at all times (R)
	Q34	Government departments ensure that employees have the knowledge to answer citizens' questions
	Q35	Government departments make sure that employees give personal attention to all
	Q36	Government departments make sure that employees understand citizens' needs

(continued)

(continued)

Construct	No.	Questions
TRANSF	Q37	In Government Departments new ideas are readily accepted
	Q38	In Government Departments management is quick to spot the need to do things differently
	Q39	In Government Departments response is quick when changes need to be made
	Q40	In Government Departments there is flexibility; they can quickly change procedures to meet new conditions and solve problems as they arise
	Q41	In Government Departments assistance in developing new ideas is readily available
PERFO	Q42	The performance of the e-government services related to finding information is excellent (e-information)
	Q43	The performance of the e-government services related to completing transactions is efficient (e-transaction)
	Q44	The performance related to public participating electronically is noticeable and visible (e-participation)
	Q45	The overall performance of e-government services (e-performance) is effective and efficient
SATISF	Q46	I was satisfied with my experience when using e-government services while looking for information I needed (e-information)
	Q47	I was satisfied with the experience I had while completing my e-government services transactions (e-transaction)
	Q48	I was satisfied with the extent of my participating as a citizen electronically (e-participation)
	Q49	I was satisfied with the extent of e-government services provided through multiple channels (e.g. websites; kiosks and mobile phones)
	Q50	Overall I was satisfied with the services provided electronically (e-performance)
TRU_COF	Q51	I feel that government acts in citizen's best interest
	Q52	I feel fine interacting with the government since government generally fulfills its duties efficiently
	Q53	I am comfortable relying on the government to meet their obligations
	Q54	I always feel confident that I can rely on government to do their part when I interact with them
	Q55	I feel confident that the government department will do a good job providing the services that I used in the future

Appendix B
Research Instruments (Main Survey)

Construct	Measuring items	
EGOV	Q1	People would learn to use the government departments' website very quickly
	Q2	I found information on the government departments' website to be very useful
	Q3	I found helpful features on the government departments' website for accomplishing my task
	Q4	Through every step of navigation through the website, I found the government departments' website to consistently provide useful information
	Q5	I found that the content in the government departments' website was organized appropriately
	Q6	I found the design of the government departments' website visually pleasing
	Q7	I found that various within the government department were properly not linked together
	Q8	I was able to save the transaction details for future reference
	Q9	I was able to choose the manner in which I am sent reminders/notifications about my transaction
	Q10	I was able to request for accessing information the way I wanted to (i.e. on mobile devices or electronic mail) on the days I wanted to
TRANSPY	Q11	The government departments' programs are implemented more transparently in the website
	Q12	The government departments' decision making is transparently disclosed in the website
	Q13	The citizen can clearly see the progress and situation of the decision making through the website
	Q14	The government departments' website discloses sufficient and reliable information to the citizen on its policies

(continued)

M. Mahmood, *Does Digital Transformation of Government Lead to Enhanced Citizens' Trust and Confidence in Government?*, Springer Theses,
https://doi.org/10.1007/978-3-030-01759-0

(continued)

Construct	Measuring items	
ACOUNT	Q15	The government departments recognise their responsibilities towards all communities
	Q16	The government departments maintain detailed and up-to-date records
	Q17	The government departments foster collaboration with other related agencies
	Q18	The government departments ensure funds are used properly and in an authorized manner
TECH	Q19	The government departments use computer networks to connect all of its divisions
	Q20	The government departments are keen on providing network security in order to secure the information
	Q21	Data exchange is conducted with great ease among the government departments' divisions through the available means of communication
EXPEC	Q22	The government departments show sincere interest in solving citizens' problems
	Q23	The government departments provide services at the time promised
	Q24	The government departments maintain error-free records
	Q25	The government departments inform citizens when services will be performed
	Q26	The government departments offer prompt services to citizens
	Q27	The government departments readily respond to citizens' request
	Q28	The government departments able to instill confidence in citizens
	Q29	The government departments ensure that citizens feel safe in their transactions
	Q30	The government departments ensure that employees have the knowledge to answer citizens' questions
	Q31	The government departments make sure that employees give personal attention to all
	Q32	The government departments make sure that employees understand citizens' needs
TRANSF	Q33	In government departments new ideas are readily accepted
	Q34	In government departments management is quick to spot the need to do things differently
	Q35	In government departments response is quick when changes need to be made
	Q36	In government departments there is flexibility; they can quickly change procedures to meet new conditions and solve problems as they arise
	Q37	In government departments assistance in developing new ideas is readily available

(continued)

(continued)

Construct	Measuring items	
PERFO	Q38	The performance of the e-government services related to finding information is excellent
	Q39	The performance of the e-government services related to completing transactions is efficient
	Q40	The performance related to public participating electronically is noticeable and visible
	Q41	The overall performance of e-government services is effective and efficient
SATISF	Q42	I was satisfied with my experience when using e-government services while looking for information I needed
	Q43	I was satisfied with the experience I had while completing my e-government services transactions
	Q44	I was satisfied with the extent of my participating as a citizen electronically
	Q45	I was satisfied with the extent of e-government services provided through multiple channels
	Q46	overall I was satisfied with the services provided electronically
TRU & COF	Q47	I feel that government acts in citizen's best interest
	Q48	I feel fine interacting with the government since government generally fulfills its duties efficiently
	Q49	I am comfortable relying on the government to meet their obligations
	Q50	I always feel confident that I can rely on government to do their part when I interact with them
	Q51	I feel confident that the government department will do a good job providing the services that I used in the future

Appendix C
Research Instruments (Following Deletion of Q7)

Construct	Measuring items	
EGOV	Q1	People would learn to use the government departments' website very quickly
	Q2	I found information on the government departments' website to be very useful
	Q3	I found helpful features on the government departments' website for accomplishing my task
	Q4	Through every step of navigation through the website, I found the government departments' website to consistently provide useful information
	Q5	I found that the content in the government departments' website was organized appropriately
	Q6	I found the design of the government departments' website visually pleasing
	Q7	I was able to save the transaction details for future reference
	Q8	I was able to choose the manner in which I am sent reminders/notifications about my transaction
	Q9	I was able to request for accessing information the way I wanted to (i.e. on mobile devices or electronic mail) on the days I wanted to
TRANSPY	Q10	The government departments' programs are implemented more transparently in the website
	Q11	The government departments' decision making is transparently disclosed in the website
	Q12	The citizen can clearly see the progress and situation of the decision making through the website
	Q13	The government departments' website discloses sufficient and reliable information to the citizen on its policies

(continued)

M. Mahmood, *Does Digital Transformation of Government Lead to Enhanced Citizens' Trust and Confidence in Government?*, Springer Theses,
https://doi.org/10.1007/978-3-030-01759-0

(continued)

Construct	Measuring items	
ACOUNT	Q14	The government departments recognise their responsibilities towards all communities
	Q15	The government departments maintain detailed and up-to-date records
	Q16	The government departments foster collaboration with other related agencies
	Q17	The government departments ensure funds are used properly and in an authorized manner
TECH	Q18	The government departments use computer networks to connect all of its divisions
	Q19	The government departments are keen on providing network security in order to secure the information
	Q20	Data exchange is conducted with great ease among the government departments' divisions through the available means of communication
EXPEC	Q21	The government departments show sincere interest in solving citizens' problems
	Q22	The government departments provide services at the time promised
	Q23	The government departments maintain error-free records
	Q24	The government departments inform citizens when services will be performed
	Q25	The government departments offer prompt services to citizens
	Q26	The government departments readily respond to citizens' request
	Q27	The government departments able to instill confidence in citizens
	Q28	The government departments ensure that citizens feel safe in their transactions
	Q29	The government departments ensure that employees have the knowledge to answer citizens' questions
	Q30	The government departments make sure that employees give personal attention to all
	Q31	The government departments make sure that employees understand citizens' needs
TRANSF	Q32	In government departments new ideas are readily accepted
	Q33	In government departments management is quick to spot the need to do things differently.
	Q34	In government departments response is quick when changes need to be made
	Q35	In government departments there is flexibility; they can quickly change procedures to meet new conditions and solve problems as they arise
	Q36	In government departments assistance in developing new ideas is readily available

(continued)

(continued)

Construct	Measuring items	
PERFO	Q37	The performance of the e-government services related to finding information is excellent
	Q38	The performance of the e-government services related to completing transactions is efficient
	Q39	The performance related to public participating electronically is noticeable and visible
	Q40	The overall performance of e-government services is effective and efficient
SATISF	Q41	I was satisfied with my experience when using e-government services while looking for information I needed
	Q42	I was satisfied with the experience I had while completing my e-government services transactions
	Q43	I was satisfied with the extent of my participating as a citizen electronically
	Q44	I was satisfied with the extent of e-government services provided through multiple channels
	Q45	Overall I was satisfied with the services provided electronically
TRU & COF	Q46	I feel that government acts in citizen's best interest
	Q47	I feel fine interacting with the government since government generally fulfills its duties efficiently
	Q48	I am comfortable relying on the government to meet their obligations
	Q49	I always feel confident that I can rely on government to do their part when I interact with them
	Q50	I feel confident that the government department will do a good job providing the services that I used in the future

Appendix D Research Instruments (After Data Analysis)

Construct	Measuring items	
EGOV	Q1	People would learn to use the government departments' website very quickly
	Q2	I found information on the government departments' website to be very useful
	Q3	I found helpful features on the government departments' website for accomplishing my task
	Q4	Through every step of navigation through the website, I found the government departments' website to consistently provide useful information
	Q5	I found that the content in the government departments' website was organized appropriately
	Q6	I found the design of the government departments' website visually pleasing
TRANSPY	Q7	The government departments' programs are implemented more transparently in the website
	Q8	The government departments' decision making is transparently disclosed in the website
	Q9	The citizen can clearly see the progress and situation of the decision making through the website
	Q10	The government departments' website discloses sufficient and reliable information to the citizen on its policies
ACOUNT	Q11	The government departments recognise their responsibilities towards all communities
	Q12	The government departments maintain detailed and up-to-date records
	Q13	The government departments foster collaboration with other related agencies
	Q14	The government departments ensure funds are used properly and in an authorized manner

(continued)

M. Mahmood, *Does Digital Transformation of Government Lead to Enhanced Citizens' Trust and Confidence in Government?*, Springer Theses,
https://doi.org/10.1007/978-3-030-01759-0

(continued)

Construct	Measuring items	
TECH	Q15	The government departments use computer networks to connect all of its divisions
	Q16	The government departments are keen on providing network security in order to secure the information
	Q17	Data exchange is conducted with great ease among the government departments' divisions through the available means of communication
EXPEC	Q18	The government departments show sincere interest in solving citizens' problems
	Q19	The government departments provide services at the time promised
	Q20	The government departments maintain error-free records
	Q21	The government departments inform citizens when services will be performed
	Q22	The government departments offer prompt services to citizens
	Q23	The government departments readily respond to citizens' request
	Q24	The government departments able to instill confidence in citizens
	Q25	The government departments ensure that citizens feel safe in their transactions
	Q26	The government departments ensure that employees have the knowledge to answer citizens' questions
	Q27	The government departments make sure that employees give personal attention to all
	Q28	The government departments make sure that employees understand citizens' needs
TRANSF	Q29	In government departments new ideas are readily accepted
	Q30	In government departments management is quick to spot the need to do things differently
	Q31	In government departments response is quick when changes need to be made
	Q32	In government departments there is flexibility; they can quickly change procedures to meet new conditions and solve problems as they arise
	Q33	In government departments assistance in developing new ideas is readily available
PERFO	Q34	The performance of the e-government services related to finding information is excellent
	Q35	The performance of the e-government services related to completing transactions is efficient
	Q36	The performance related to public participating electronically is noticeable and visible
	Q37	The overall performance of e-government services is effective and efficient

(continued)

(continued)

Construct	Measuring items	
SATISF	Q38	I was satisfied with my experience when using e-government services while looking for information I needed
	Q39	I was satisfied with the experience I had while completing my e-government services transactions
	Q40	I was satisfied with the extent of my participating as a citizen electronically
	Q41	I was satisfied with the extent of e-government services provided through multiple channels (e.g. websites; kiosks and mobile phones)
	Q42	Overall I was satisfied with the services provided electronically
TRU & COF	Q43	I feel that government acts in citizen's best interest
	Q44	I feel fine interacting with the government since government generally fulfills its duties efficiently
	Q45	I am comfortable relying on the government to meet their obligations
	Q46	I always feel confident that I can rely on government to do their part when I interact with them
	Q47	I feel confident that the government department will do a good job providing the services that I used in the future

Appendix E
Research Ethics Approval

College of Business, Arts and Social Sciences Research Ethics Committee
Brunel University London
Kingston Lane
Uxbridge
UB8 3PH
United Kingdom

www.brunel.ac.uk

23 September 2015

LETTER OF APPROVAL

Applicant: Mr Mohamed Mahmood

Project Title: Citizens' trust in government

Reference: 0196-LR-Sep/2015-60

Dear Mr Mohamed Mahmood

The Research Ethics Committee has considered the above application recently submitted by you.

The Chair, acting under delegated authority, is satisfied that the amendments accord with the decision of the Committee and has agreed that there is no objection on ethical grounds to the proposed study. Approval is given on the understanding that the conditions of approval set out below are followed:

- The agreed protocol must be followed. Any changes to the protocol will require prior approval from the Committee.

Please note that:

- Research Participant Information Sheets and (where relevant) flyers, posters, and consent forms should include a clear statement that research ethics approval has been obtained from the relevant Research Ethics Committee.
- The Research Participant Information Sheets should include a clear statement that queries should be directed, in the first instance, to the Supervisor (where relevant), or the researcher. Complaints, on the other hand, should be directed, in the first instance, to the Chair of the relevant Research Ethics Committee
- Approval to proceed with the study is granted subject to receipt by the Committee of satisfactory responses to any conditions that may appear above, in addition to any subsequent changes to the protocol.
- The Research Ethics Committee reserves the right to sample and review documentation, including raw data, relevant to the study.
- You may not undertake any research activity if you are not a registered student of Brunel University or if you cease to become registered, including abeyance or temporary withdrawal. As a deregistered student you would not be insured to undertake research activity. Research activity includes the recruitment of participants, undertaking consent procedures and collection of data. Breach of this requirement constitutes research misconduct and is a disciplinary offence.

Professor James Knowles

Chair

College of Business, Arts and Social Sciences Research Ethics Committee
Brunel University London

Page 1 of 1

M. Mahmood, *Does Digital Transformation of Government Lead to Enhanced Citizens' Trust and Confidence in Government?*, Springer Theses,
https://doi.org/10.1007/978-3-030-01759-0

MIX
Papier aus verantwortungsvollen Quellen
Paper from responsible sources
FSC® C105338

If you have any concerns about our products,
you can contact us on
ProductSafety@springernature.com

In case Publisher is established outside the EU,
the EU authorized representative is:
Springer Nature Customer Service Center GmbH
Europaplatz 3, 69115 Heidelberg, Germany

Printed by Libri Plureos GmbH
in Hamburg, Germany